ESSENTIAL
STRENGTH
TRAINING
SKILLS

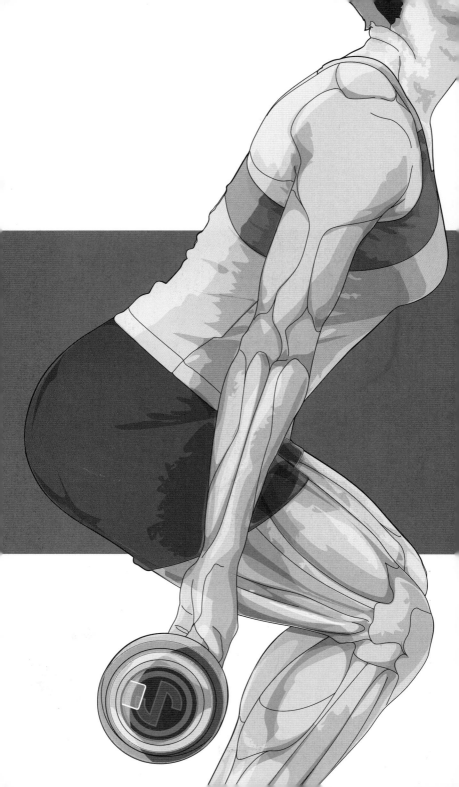

ESSENTIAL
STRENGTH
TRAINING
SKILLS

KEY TIPS AND TECHNIQUES
TO IMPROVE YOUR PHYSIQUE

Includes content previously published in
Strength Training

LONDON, NEW YORK, MUNICH,
MELBOURNE, DELHI

Senior Editor	Bob Bridle
Senior Art Editor	Sharon Spencer
Production Editor	Tony Phipps
Production Controller	Louise Minihane
Jacket Designer	Mark Cavanagh
Managing Editor	Stephanie Farrow
Managing Art Editor	Lee Griffiths
US Editor	Margaret Parrish

DK INDIA

Managing Art Editor	Ashita Murgai
Editorial Lead	Saloni Talwar
Senior Art Editor	Rajnish Kashyap
Project Designer	Pooja Pipil
Project Editor	Neha Gupta
Designers	Akanksha Gupta, Diya Kapur
Editors	Karishma Walia, Garima Sharma
DTP Manager	Balwant Singh
Senior DTP Designer	Harish Aggarwal
DTP Designers	Shanker Prasad, Anita Yadav, Vishal Bhatia
Managing Director	Aparna Sharma

First American Edition, 2011

Published in the United States by
DK Publishing
375 Hudson Street
New York, New York 10014
11 12 13 14 15 10 9 8 7 6 5 4 3 2 1

001—179529—Mar/2011

Includes content previously published in
Strength Training

A catalog record for this book
is available from the Library of Congress

ISBN 978-0-7566-7173-0

DK books are available at special discounts when
purchased in bulk for sales promotions, premiums,
fund raising, or educational use. For details, contact:
DK Publishing Special Markets, 375 Hudson Street,
New York, New York 10014 or SpecialSales@dk.com.

Printed and bound by
L. Rex Printing Company Limited, China

Discover more at www.dk.com

Contents

Introduction

Strength training is an increasingly popular activity among men and women of all ages, and offers you a wealth of health benefits—from bigger muscles to stronger bones to increased confidence. With so much conflicting information available, however, how can you be sure that you are getting the best out of your training?

This authoritative, comprehensive, and beautifully illustrated guide is written by strength training experts with more than thirty years' experience of coaching. It contains everything you need to know to get the very best from your regimen, whether you want to develop your strength, build your physique, or are training for specific gains within a chosen sport or activity.

The first chapter, The Basics, provides you with all the basic nuts-and-bolts information about how strength training works, and the best ways to achieve your goals, whether you are an experienced gym user, or a complete novice.

The main section of the book covers more than 70 exercises in detail, working through the whole body systematically, with separate sections on the warm-up and the cool-down.

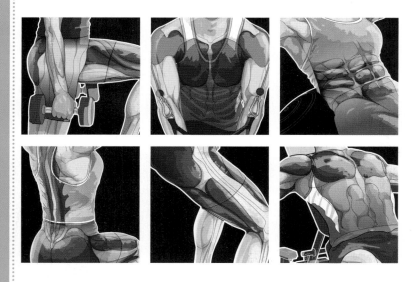

The exercises feature miniature anatomical artworks to show you the target muscles—the muscles you are working. Next to the anatomical artwork, you will find a difficulty indicator; the greater the number of red bars shown on the indicator, the harder the exercise. You are guided through each movement with clear step-by-step artworks, which show you how to perform the exercise with optimum technique. Finally, you are offered a range of helpful features such as variations, or tips for avoiding common mistakes to keep you safe and maximize the effectiveness of your training. Also, should you know what a particular exercise looks like but not what it's called, you can locate it using the Exercise Gallery on pages 8–11.

The final section offers a pragmatic, no-nonsense approach to the subject of training programs. It includes a range of specially commissioned goal-based examples to suit your needs, whatever your goals or experience, along with useful information on the key exercises for specific sports, to help you tailor your training to suit a particular activity.

WARNING

All sports and physical activity involves some risk of injury. Please check the safety information on p.176 before embarking on any of the exercises or programs shown in this book.

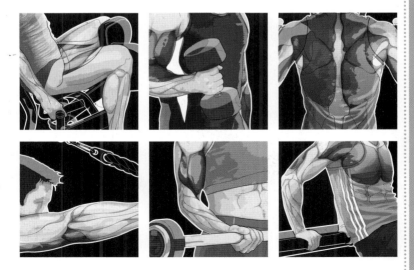

Exercise gallery

Push-up
p.52

Frame-supported
push-up p.53

Machine bench
press p.54

Machine fly
p.55

CHEST

Cable cross-over
pp.56–57

Barbell bench
press p.58

Dumbbell bench
press p.59

Incline barbell
bench press p.60

Incline dumbbell
bench press p.61

Incline fly
pp.62–63

Chin-up
pp.64–65

Back extension
p.66

BACK

Seated pulley row
p.67

Standing pulley
row p.68

Lat pull-down
p.69

Assisted chin-up
p.70

Straight-arm
pull-down p.71

Prone row
p.72

One-arm row
p.73

Bent-over row
pp.74–75

Barbell pull-over
pp.76–77

Bench dip
p.78

Bar dip
p.79

Pulley curl
p.80

ARMS

Reverse pulley curl p.81

Triceps push-down
p.82

Overhead triceps extension p.83

Wrist extension
p.84

Wrist flexion
p.85

Barbell curl
p.86

Preacher curl
p.87

Hammer dumbbell curl p.88

Incline dumbbell curl p.89

Dumbbell triceps extension p.90

Barbell triceps extension p.91

Close-grip bench press pp.92–93

Prone triceps extension p.94

Triceps kickback
p.95

Front dumbbell raise p.96

Lateral dumbbell raise p.97

SHOULDERS

Military barbell press p.98

Dumbbell shoulder press p.99

Upright row pp.100–01

Rear lateral raise pp.102–03

Squat p.104

Forward lunge p.105

45-degree leg press p.106

Calf raise p.107

LEGS

Machine leg extension p.108

Machine leg curl p.109

Back squat p.110

Front barbell squat p.111

Barbell deadlift pp.112–13

Overhead barbell lunge p.114

Straight-leg deadlift p.115

Dumbbell split squat p.116

Overhead split squat p.117

Barbell step-up pp.118–19

Bulgarian barbell split squat p.120

Good morning barbell p.121

Power clean
pp.122–23

Power snatch
pp.124–25

Abdominal crunch
p.126

Sit-up
p.127

CORE AND ABS

Reverse crunch
p.128

90-90 crunch
p.129

Figure-4 crunch
p.130

V-leg raise
p.131

Prone plank
p.132

Side plank
p.133

Roman chair side
bend p.134

Ball crunch
p.135

Ball twist
p.136

Ball back extension
p.137

Ball press-up
p.138

Ball jackknife
p.139

Woodchop
pp.140–41

Side bend
p.142

Suitcase deadlift
p.143

Anatomical chart

ANTERIOR MUSCLES

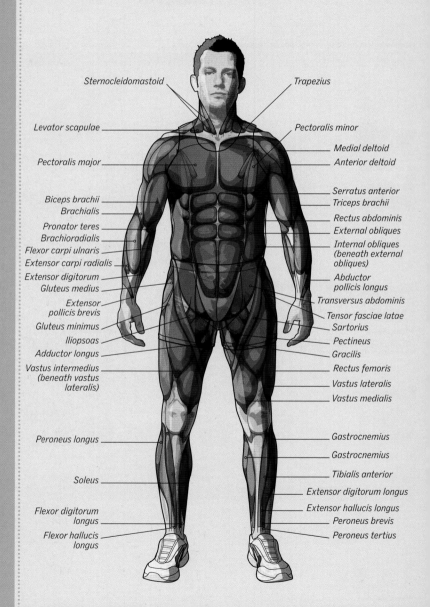

Sternocleidomastoid

Trapezius

Levator scapulae

Pectoralis minor

Medial deltoid

Anterior deltoid

Pectoralis major

Biceps brachii

Serratus anterior

Brachialis

Triceps brachii

Pronator teres

Rectus abdominis

Brachioradialis

External obliques

Flexor carpi ulnaris

Internal obliques
(beneath external
obliques)

Extensor carpi radialis

Extensor digitorum

Abductor
pollicis longus

Gluteus medius

Extensor
pollicis brevis

Transversus abdominis

Gluteus minimus

Tensor fasciae latae

Iliopsoas

Sartorius

Adductor longus

Pectineus

Vastus intermedius
(beneath vastus
lateralis)

Gracilis

Rectus femoris

Vastus lateralis

Vastus medialis

Peroneus longus

Gastrocnemius

Gastrocnemius

Tibialis anterior

Soleus

Extensor digitorum longus

Flexor digitorum
longus

Extensor hallucis longus

Peroneus brevis

Flexor hallucis
longus

Peroneus tertius

POSTERIOR MUSCLES

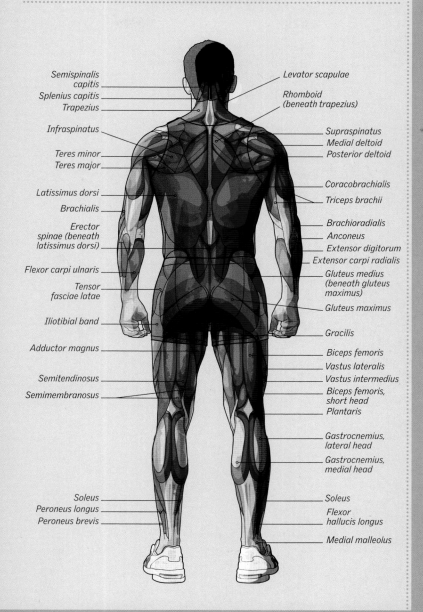

Semispinalis capitis
Splenius capitis
Trapezius
Infraspinatus
Teres minor
Teres major
Latissimus dorsi
Brachialis
Erector spinae (beneath latissimus dorsi)
Flexor carpi ulnaris
Tensor fasciae latae
Iliotibial band
Adductor magnus
Semitendinosus
Semimembranosus
Soleus
Peroneus longus
Peroneus brevis

Levator scapulae
Rhomboid (beneath trapezius)
Supraspinatus
Medial deltoid
Posterior deltoid
Coracobrachialis
Triceps brachii
Brachioradialis
Anconeus
Extensor digitorum
Extensor carpi radialis
Gluteus medius (beneath gluteus maximus)
Gluteus maximus
Gracilis
Biceps femoris
Vastus lateralis
Vastus intermedius
Biceps femoris, short head
Plantaris
Gastrocnemius, lateral head
Gastrocnemius, medial head
Soleus
Flexor hallucis longus
Medial malleolus

The Basics

What are your goals?

Some of you will have picked up this book because you want greater strength and physical power, perhaps to boost self-confidence, to ease day-to-day activities, to prevent injury, or to improve your posture. It may be that you are not happy with your appearance and desire a more muscular, defined body—that elusive concept of looking more "toned." Your primary goal may be to improve your performance in a particular sport, or you may be intrigued by the challenges of the strength sports—weightlifting and powerlifting.

Bodybuilding and strength training

Bodybuilding differs from strength training in that its primary goals are to maximize muscle mass (promote hypertrophy) while reducing body fat, so sculpting your physique. It is a cosmetic activity, in which any gain in strength or power is a by-product.

On the positive side, bodybuilding has undoubtedly inspired many people to get involved in strength training and to think about improving their fitness. The sport certainly provides some spectacular visuals, especially at the highest competitive levels. However, for every person who is enthralled at the prospect of huge biceps, there is another whose primary goal is to simply keep his or her body healthy.

Training for the sport of life

You may not want to be a bodybuilder, weightlifter, or powerlifter. Instead you may simply want to look a bit better, increase your muscle mass a small amount, and reduce your body fat levels. Perhaps you want to be able to cope better with the demands of daily life and be able to continue to do this effectively well into old age. Resistance training can assist you in achieving any or all of these goals.

Training for sports

Athletes need to engage in strength and power training to enhance their sporting performance. Sport-specific conditioning may include aspects of general strength training (including those with a physiotherapy slant), weightlifting, powerlifting, and even bodybuilding (in sports where gains in bodyweight and muscle mass may be of benefit).

WHAT IS STRENGTH TRAINING?

The term "strength training" is often used interchangeably with "resistance training" and "weight training" but they are not synonymous.

Resistance training is any form of exercise that causes muscles to contract against an external resistance. Weights are just one tool: you can use rubber or elastic bands, your own bodyweight, cables, hydraulics, water, a partner, or even a vibration platform to provide resistance.

Strength training is any form of resistance training engaged in to enhance muscle strength.

Weight training is any form of resistance training where weights are used to provide resistance and challenge your strength.

Strength sports

Another aspect of strength training is participation in the two strength sports of weightlifting and powerlifting. The object in both is to lift as much weight as physically possible, in particular styles of lift, for one repetition.

Weightlifting

It features two lifts—the snatch, and the clean and jerk. In snatch, the objective is to lift weight overhead, quickly in one movement; in the clean and jerk, two movements are utilized. Though weightlifting itself is a sport, techniques of the clean and jerk and the snatch are used in sport-specific strength training and general strength training.

Powerlifting

It comprises the lifts of the bench press, squat, and deadlift. Ironically, powerlifting requires a large amount of pure strength but little explosive power, because the lifts are completed with incredibly heavy weights that can be moved only very slowly. Elite powerlifters are arguably the strongest athletes in the world.

ONE SIZE DOESN'T FIT ALL

To succeed in any training program, you should have a clear idea of what you want to achieve, where you are starting from, and who you are. The responses of two people to the same training program are likely to be very different depending on the following factors:

Chronological age	Age in years.
Biological age	Age in relation to physical maturity—especially important for trainees in their early- to mid-teens.
Training age	Age in relation to the number of years of experience of training with weights and of sport in general.
Emotional maturity	Ability to concentrate during training and handle the fact that results may sometimes be elusive.
Gender	Men and women respond differently to strength training in both physiological and psychological terms.
Physical capability	Affected by both heredity (see below) and training history (degree of skill and fitness developed).
Heredity	Some people have innate strength, or can add bone and muscle mass more quickly than others; the distinct fibers in your skeletal muscles and some aspects of personality are also genetically determined.
Lifestyle	The degree to which training programs can be fit into life outside the gym.

Having a firm grip on your goals is vital to developing an effective resistance training program that will, in the long run, leave you feeling satisfied with your achievements.

Planning your training

Elite athletes work with their coaches to develop sophisticated training programs that run over months or years, manipulating intensities and loading patterns so that the athlete reaches peak performance at just the right time. But even if you are a recreational trainee, some degree of planning is highly desirable. Your body will respond optimally to training only if it is subjected to progressive overload at the right volume, intensity, and frequency, allowing sufficient periods for recovery between your sessions.

> ❝ ALWAYS SUBJECT YOUR BODY TO **PROGRESSIVE OVERLOAD** AT THE RIGHT **VOLUME**, **INTENSITY**, AND **FREQUENCY**. ❞

KEY TERMS	
The world of strength training has its own jargon, so before considering the subject of planning, let's introduce some key concepts and terms that are used in the area.	
Weight/mass	The weight to be lifted.
Repetition (or "rep")	Each time a weight is lifted is termed a repetition, or a rep for short.
Set	Groups of repetitions are organized into sets. You could, for example, perform three sets of 10 repetitions.
1RM (one repetition maximum)	The maximum amount of weight you can lift in a single repetition of a given exercise.
%1RM	The percentage of your 1RM that a weight represents: if the maximum weight you can lift for a single repetition is 220lb (100kg), a weight of 175lb (80kg) represents 80% of 1RM.
Inter-set rest period/interval	The time spent recovering between sets—usually seconds or minutes.
Inter-session rest period/interval	The amount of time spent recovering between sessions. Usually hours or days.
Work-to-rest ratio	The ratio of the time spent active during a set to the time spent recovering between sets. For example, if a set takes 20 seconds and you recover for 3 minutes, that is a work-to-rest ratio of 1:9. Basically, the lower the %1RM lifted, the lower the inter-set rest period required.

Training intensity and volume

Q | WHAT SHOULD BE MY TRAINING INTENSITY?

A | The greater the load lifted, the greater is your training intensity. Intensity is commonly expressed as a percentage of your one repetition maximum (see box, opposite). Opinions vary, but it is generally assumed that an intensity of more than 70–80% 1RM is required to enhance strength.

Often you will see programs described in terms of %1RM (see box, opposite), although you will also see terms such as 3RM and 10RM; your 3RM is the weight you can lift a maximum of three times and your 10RM is the weight you can lift a maximum of 10 times before your muscles fail: these are often a more useful measure than the 1RM.

To measure your 1RM for a particular exercise, first warm up, then choose and lift a weight that is achievable. After a rest of at least a few minutes, increase the weight and try again. Repeat until you arrive at the heaviest weight that you can lift while still maintaining good form. This is your 1RM. Be sure to progress to the maximum weight without prior fatigue to your muscles.

Q | HOW DOES TRAINING VOLUME AFFECT MY TRAINING?

A | Training volume is the total amount of weight shifted in a workout—the load multiplied by the number of reps and sets carried out. The relationship between intensity and volume is not straightforward. Typically, as you increase intensity, you will decrease volume, and vice versa. Training at a high volume, with lots of reps and sets performed with comfortable weights, is an excellent way to learn movements, but if you avoid more challenging loads you will not develop power and strength.

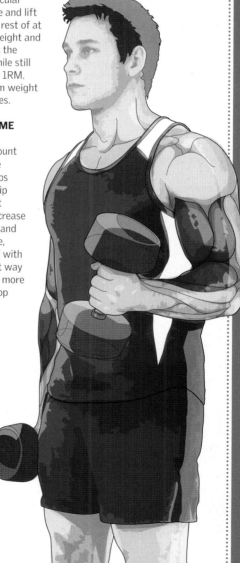

> **❝** TRAINING AT A **HIGH VOLUME** WITH LOTS OF **REPS AND SETS** IS AN EXCELLENT WAY TO LEARN MOVEMENTS. **❞**

Basic planning principles

Here are five basic pieces of advice to follow when
you plan your strength training program.

1. SELECT EFFECTIVE EXERCISES

Put large, multi-joint, compound
exercises at the core of your
workout. Exercises such as squats,
deadlifts, bench presses, chin-ups
and pull-ups, bent-over rows, and
standing shoulder presses work
the largest amounts of muscle mass
and are associated with a hormone
response that is key to muscle
growth. Avoid doing three, four,
or five separate exercises that
target one body part; such multiple
exercises will batter your muscles
into submission, rather than
stimulating them into more growth.

2. REST MORE THAN YOU TRAIN

Don't get caught up in the macho
mindset of feeling you have to live
in the gym. If you do key exercises
given on the box on the opposite
page twice a week, you will get
great results. In fact, you can
expect even better results than
doing it four times a week or doing
a routine that has you in the gym
almost daily, performing multiple
exercises per body part. Remember
that you grow while resting—the
time you spend in the gym just
provides the impetus for growth.

5. PROGRESS LOADS SLOWLY

Progressive overloading of your
muscles is key to developing
strength. However, when working
at high intensities, you will not be
able to add large amounts of weight
at every workout. The smallest plate
in most gyms weighs $2^1/_2$lb (1.25kg),
which means the smallest jump you
can make on a barbell is 5lb (2.5kg).
If you are able to bench press 165lb
(75kg) for 10 repetitions, an addition
of 5lb (2.5kg) equates to a load
increase of around 3 percent. If you
could add this amount to your bench
press every session, for two sessions
per week, and for one year, you would
be bench pressing 737lb (335kg) for
10 repetitions, making you one of
the strongest people in the world! For
a standard-diameter weight training
bar it is easy to find $1^1/_4$lb (0.5kg)

plates, but they are also available for
Olympic-size bars. Even a gradual
increase of just $1^1/_4$–$2^1/_2$lb (0.5–1kg)
per week on your lifts will result in a
gain of between 57 and 115lb (26 and
52kg) per year. That gain is immense.

Smaller jumps are more sustainable. If
you cannot find small plates, there is
another technique for progression
that works well. Imagine you can
perform 10 repetitions of a shoulder
press with 35lb (16kg) dumbbells and
you decide to progress the weight to
40lb (18kg). You are very unlikely
to be able to perform 10 repetitions
with the new weight right away.
Instead, you should try progressing
loads slowly. If your rate of adaptation
outstrips the weekly weight increase,
then try jumping by two reps per week.

3. DON'T OVERDO THE SETS

For the everyman or woman, performing many sets per exercise or body part is counterproductive. Your goal should be to stimulate growth, then put the barbell down and step away from it. You should do a couple of warm-up sets, followed by two, or at the most three, actual work sets.

4. ALTERNATE TRAINING

Muscular failure is the point at which you are no longer able to perform another repetition with the weight that you are lifting. It is therefore advisable that you alternate periods of training to muscular failure with periods of working within your comfort zone. It is believed that training to failure, when done to excess, is likely to become detrimental to your strength. In strength training, the point at which your movement becomes shaky and irregular is called "being on the nerve." You should try to be just shy of this point.

KEY EXERCISES FOR A SIMPLE PROGRAM	
Chest and triceps	Bench presses
Back and biceps	Pull-ups or bent-over rows
Legs and lower back	Squats or deadlifts
Shoulders	Standing shoulder presses
Biceps	Standing biceps curls
Triceps	Close-grip bench presses

EXERCISES, REPETITIONS, AND SETS	
Chest and triceps	Bench press: 2–3 sets of 10 reps
Back and biceps	Bent-over row: 2–3 sets of 10 reps
Legs and lower back	Back squat: 2–3 sets of 10 reps
Shoulders	Standing shoulder press: 2–3 sets of 10 reps
Biceps	Standing biceps curl: 2–3 sets of 10 reps
Triceps	Close-grip bench press: 2–3 sets of 10 reps

Sports-specific training

It is widely accepted today that athletes need to engage in some form of strength training to enhance their sporting performance. However, the needs of a football player are obviously different from those of a swimmer, and a cyclist will not benefit from a program designed for a baseball player. The key point is that strength training for athletes must be specific to the demands of their sport.

❝ STRENGTH TRAINING FOR ATHLETES MUST BE **SPECIFIC TO THE DEMANDS OF THEIR SPORT**: YOU SHOULD TRAIN MOVEMENTS, NOT MUSCLES. **❞**

STRENGTH TRAINING ATTRIBUTES	
Athletes will need to develop some of the following attributes through strength training:	
Explosive power	Think of a sprinter or a tennis player. Success in these and many other sports depends more on explosive power than it does upon pure, slow strength.
Muscular endurance	Think of a rower or a cyclist. In sports like these, the ability to generate a moderate force over a prolonged period is far more important than being able to exert a huge force for a short period of time.
Maximal strength	Think of a powerlifter, who needs to exert an enormous amount of force for one repetition. Here, pure strength is the key determinant of success. Similarly, members of the defensive line of a football team also require high levels of pure strength to push against a strong opposition line. You should also not neglect the importance of pure strength to power output. Power (P) is a product of the force applied (F) and the velocity (V), or speed, at which it is applied: $P = F \times V$. If the force applied is low, power will always be low. For this reason, weightlifters wishing to develop their power will train for a high level of pure strength. Maximal strength is also very relevant to muscular endurance. The more weight you can lift in a single repetition, the less challenging any given force will be. So if your 1RM for the bench press is 660lb (300kg), you will be able to perform many more repetitions with 220lb (100kg) than someone with a 265lb (120kg) 1RM.
Hypertrophy	Think of a football player or a rugby player. For these athletes, sheer muscular bulk is required to counter aggressive body contact. However, for athletes in other sports, too much bulk can be a hindrance.

Train movements, not muscles

For bodybuilding and recreational training, a muscle-centered approach may make some sense, but not for enhancing sporting performance.

Sports are all about movement, and your training should address your ability to perform movements more effectively, efficiently, and powerfully. Simply maximizing strength in the muscles involved in a movement, but in an isolated fashion, does not maximize strength development in that movement. For instance, to become stronger in squatting movements, you need to squat.

To become more powerful in rotation, you need to rotate powerfully. It is common sense.

The reason for this is that the development of coordination (both within and between muscles), skill learning, and the adaptation of your nervous system to the movement patterns trained, plays huge roles in the development of strength in movements. Unless you give your body opportunities to do a movement, it has only limited ability to improve at it. All this leads us to the inevitable conclusion: train movements, not muscles.

General sports movements

Although each sport has its own specific movements, different sports have similarities in terms of the movements they require. Most team games, for example, involve triple extension through the hip, knee, and ankle (the motion required for jumping and straight-line acceleration), single leg strength and power (for running,

changing direction, etc.), strength and stability through the core and pillar, trunk rotation, and so on. This means that sports can be broken down into the types of general movement that need to be trained, such as rotation, triple extension, push, pull, squat, as opposed to treating each sport as totally unique.

Functional training

Functional training is performed to make your body better at performing those movements that you will use in a particular sport or in daily life. It is at the cutting edge of preparing athletes for competition.

It is easy to start making huge distinctions between bodybuilding and athletic conditioning along the lines of nonfunctional vs. functional, but that certainly doesn't tell the full story. Yes, most bodybuilders will use exercises that isolate a muscle in a way in which it would never be used in sports performance, but many also utilize exercises, such as squats and bent-over rows, that fit into the "movements, not muscles" philosophy. The key to functional strength training is to think carefully about how applicable a particular exercise—including its rate, frequency,

and direction—is to the movements you perform on the field or on court. Sometimes this means questioning exercise orthodoxy.

Consider, for example, the abdominal crunch, which has for years had a place in almost every athlete's training program. Think about the way in which gravity loads the upper body when you perform this movement from a lying position. Then consider how dramatically this changes as soon as you are on your feet, where hip and spinal flexion require no effort at all. Unless you take part in a sport where you spend a great deal of time horizontal, such as wrestling, jiu-jitsu, and gymnastics, the crunch is of questionable functional benefit. That is not to say it is a bad exercise, but you should question its blanket use as a means of strengthening your trunk.

Warming up

Warming up and cooling down are too often overlooked in many training programs. Time pressures make it tempting to skip a warm-up, but you do so at your peril. Warming up is essential because it gets your body ready for intense work while minimizing the risk of injury and maximizing your potential to learn and improve.

Warm-up regime

A warm-up should take no longer than 20 minutes; begin by skipping, jogging, or working on a cross-trainer for 10 minutes, and then do 10 minutes of mobilization exercises (see opposite). Consistently warming up before a workout will greatly improve your level of performance.

BENEFITS OF WARMING UP
Increased heart rate to prepare you for work.
Increased blood flow through active tissues, which leads to increased metabolism.
Increased speed of contraction and relaxation of warmed muscles.
Reduction in pre-workout muscle stiffness.
Better use of oxygen by warmed muscles.
Better quality and fluency of movement from warmed muscles.
Higher temperatures, which help nerve transmission and metabolism in muscles.
Specific warm-ups can help with what physiologists call "motor unit recruitment." A motor unit consists of a nerve fiber together with all its associated muscle fibers. Warming up will increase both the number of motor units brought into play and the rate at which they fire (contract).
Increased mental focus on the training and competition.

❝ WARMING UP GETS YOUR BODY READY FOR INTENSE WORK WHILE MINIMIZING THE RISK OF INJURY. ❞

Mobilization exercises

Sometimes called dynamic stretching, or movement preparation, mobilization exercises are controlled movements, where you go through a full range of motion without stopping (see pp.36–49).

They are an ideal way to prepare for a workout because they reduce muscle stiffness and help reduce the chance of injury. As you become more advanced and flexible, you can add a controlled swing to push a body part past its usual range of movement. The force of the swing may be gradually increased but should never become too extreme.

Warm-up is not the time for static stretches (see pp.146–53)—those in which you put your body into a position where the target muscles are under tension. Using static stretches before a workout may reduce your capacity to release power and does little or nothing to minimize the chances of injury.

Cooling down

When you finish your workout, you should bring your body back down to its pre-exercise state in a controlled manner. During a workout, your body is under stress: muscles get damaged and waste products build up. A good cool-down will help your body to repair itself.

Cooling down and recovery techniques

Cooling down need not be a lengthy process: start with 5–10 minutes of gentle jogging or walking, which decreases your body temperature and helps remove the waste products from your working muscles.

Follow this with 5–10 minutes of stretches (as described on pp.146–53), which help your muscles to relax and the muscle fibers to realign and reestablish their normal range of movement. To perform the stretches, extend the target muscle(s) as far as it can comfortably go, easing into the stretch, and then hold that position for around 10 seconds.

Some suggest the cool-down phase of the workout is an ideal time for "developmental stretching," which is designed to increase muscle flexibility and your range of movement. Developmental stretches have the same form as the simple cool-down stretches: you first hold the stretch for around 10 seconds, then take the stretch a little farther—$^3/_8$–$^3/_4$in (1–2cm) will do—and then hold for another 20–30 seconds.

Others propose that stretching a muscle after exercise may increase muscle damage and delay recovery. Picture a muscle like a pair of panty hose. Following intense exercise the muscle is full of small microtears that are akin to small runs in the hose. Stretching a muscle at this point is like stretching the hose— perhaps not the best idea. A happy medium may be some light and gentle developmental stretching after your workout for muscles that feel particularly tight. Don't compare yourself to others in the gym—some people have great mobility and you could be in trouble if you try to match their range of movement.

" WHILE YOU ARE CARRYING OUT A COOL-DOWN STRETCH, YOU SHOULD **EXTEND THE TARGET MUSCLE(S)** AS FAR AS IT CAN GO, EASING INTO THE STRETCH. "

BENEFITS OF COOLING DOWN

Allows the heart rate to recover to its resting rate.

Reduces the level of adrenaline in the blood.

Potentially reduces Delayed Onset Muscle Soreness (DOMS), pain that is sometimes experienced one to three days after intense muscle activity.

Aids in the reduction of waste products in the blood, including lactic acid.

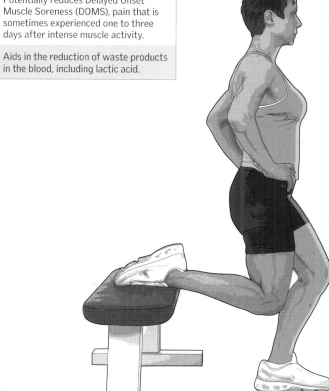

Eating right

Eating well and staying hydrated are just as important to your training plan as doing the right exercises at the right intensity and volume. The objective of a nutrition program for strength training is to develop and maintain a body with appropriate lean muscle that has the reserves of strength, power, and endurance required to meet the demands of daily life, training, and competition. The human body is a complex machine, but research has given us a good understanding of the role played by the various elements of nutrition in staying healthy, getting in shape, and in gaining and losing weight.

Proportions of main nutrients in the diet

There is no universally "correct" balance of daily nutrient intake; the proportions of the main nutrients you need depends on your individual characteristics and lifestyle. However, the following figures are a useful reference point:

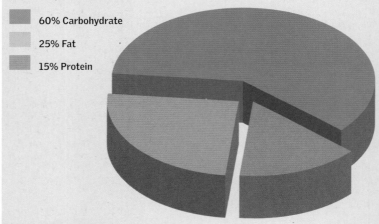

- 60% Carbohydrate
- 25% Fat
- 15% Protein

Carbohydrates (carbs)

Carbohydrates are our main source of energy. Nutritionists once distinguished between simple carbohydrates—those found in refined sugar, cookies, fruit, and fruit juices—and complex carbohydrates, found in bread, pasta, potatoes, rice, and whole-grain foods. The advice was to eat more complex and fewer simple carbohydrates because the complex ones took longer to break down and absorb and so led to fewer peaks and valleys in levels of blood sugar.

However, the relationship between carbohydrate intake and the effect on blood sugar turned out to be a little more complex. Today, it is more common to refer to foods as having a high or low glycemic index (GI). GI is a measure of the effect that a particular carbohydrate has on blood sugar levels. Low GI foods release their energy more slowly (preventing the feeling of "sugar rush") and are believed to have other health benefits (see pp.32–33).

Calories and body weight

The weight of your body is made up of your skeleton, organs, the muscle, fat, and water that the body carries. Muscular development (though not the number of muscle fibers), body fat, bone density, and the amount of water can all be changed by diet and training. The facts about weight loss and gain are simple. You gain weight if you take more calories than you burn; and lose weight if you eat fewer calories than you need to fuel your body functions and exercise regimen.

ENERGY DENSITY	
Carbohydrate	113 calories per ounce (4 calories per gram)
Protein	113 calories per ounce (4 calories per gram)
Fat	255 calories per ounce (9 calories per gram)
Water, vitamins, and minerals	Zero calorific value

Fats

Dietary fat is a rich source of energy and an essential nutrient. It enables your body to absorb vitamins and is important for proper growth, health, and development. Fat gives food much of its taste and helps you feel "full."

Not all fats are the same, and most foods contain a combination of several fats. Unsaturated fats, such as those found in oily fish, and some vegetable and nut oils are more beneficial than the saturated fats found in meat and animal products, such as butter and lard. Saturated fat in large quantities is implicated in the development of coronary heart disease and needs to be kept to the minimum in a healthy diet. Eating too much fat of any kind will lead to an increase in weight.

Proteins

The building blocks of the human body, proteins are essential to the growth and repair of body tissues. Proteins are made up of amino acids, and foods such as fish, meat, and eggs provide a complete source of amino acids. Fruit, vegetables, and nuts contain protein, but may not supply the amino acids needed by an athlete in training. So vegetarian sportsmen should take nutritional advice before embarking on high-level training.

Vitamins

Vitamins are biologically active compounds used in the chemical processes that make the human body function. Vitamins are needed only in tiny amounts and come in two types—those soluble in fat and those soluble in water (which need to be replenished regularly).

Minerals

Minerals such as potassium, sodium, calcium, zinc, and iron are involved in many biochemical processes that maintain life and fuel growth. Mineral deficiency is rare in a balanced diet.

Water

Water is crucial in maintaining health. The human body is composed largely of water and it is the medium in which most of the body's chemistry is played out. Dehydration is potentially a very serious condition and in extreme cases can lead to death.

Your energy requirements

Your Basic Energy Requirement (BER) is the amount of energy you need to maintain your basic life processes, such as breathing and circulation, when at rest. In addition to your BER, you need energy to live your lifestyle and sustain your personal work patterns. The nature of your job is important. If you do a lot of manual work, you will have a different energy requirement from someone who works at a desk all day. You can calculate your approximate daily energy requirement by using the table below.

If you take in more calories than your daily energy requirement (including the exercise you get), you will gain weight. If you take in fewer calories than your daily energy requirement (including training), you will lose weight.

CALCULATING ENERGY REQUIREMENTS

Find your age range and enter your mass into the appropriate equation to find your BER. Then, multiply this figure by the factor associated with your type of lifestyle—sedentary, moderately active, or very active. The figure you arrive at is the level of calorie intake that will allow you to maintain your present bodyweight.

SEX	AGE	WEIGHT	CALORIES
Male	10–17 years	$8 \times$ mass in lb ($17.5 \times$ mass in kg)	+ 651
	18–29 years	$7 \times$ mass in lb ($15.3 \times$ mass in kg)	+ 679
	30–59 years	$5.2 \times$ mass in lb ($11.6 \times$ mass in kg)	+ 879
Female	10–17 years	$5.5 \times$ mass in lb ($12.2 \times$ mass in kg)	+ 746
	18–29 years	$6.7 \times$ mass in lb ($14.7 \times$ mass in kg)	+ 496
	30–59 years	$4 \times$ mass in lb ($8.7 \times$ mass in kg)	+ 829
Sedentary		multiply by 1.5	
Moderately active		multiply by 1.6	
Very active		multiply by 1.7	

PLANNING YOUR TRAINING PROGRAM WITHOUT CONSIDERING YOUR DIET WILL SLOW YOUR PROGRESS, OR EVEN MAKE YOU SICK.

WHAT IS THE RIGHT LEVEL OF BODY FAT?

AVERAGE PERSON
It is generally accepted that men should have less than 18 percent of their bodyweight as fat and women 23 percent or less. A certain amount of body fat is essential to good health. There is plenty of evidence to indicate that carrying less than 5 percent body fat compromises your immune system, making you prone to illnesses and infections.

Less than 23% fat   Less than 18% fat

ATHLETES
Athletes in training, especially at the elite level, will have significantly less body fat; around 8–10 percent for men and 10–12 percent for women. High levels of fat in relative terms are a serious disadvantage to most athletes, especially in disciplines where "making weight" for a specific competitive weight class is a priority.

10–12% fat   8–10% fat

HAZARDOUS
Carrying more fat than the average person is not particularly hazardous to health until you accumulate 35 percent (men) or 40 percent (women) of total bodyweight as fat. Such levels constitute obesity and have a detrimental effect on health. Too low a level of body fat can also be hazardous, because fat is an important store of energy for aerobic activity.

40% fat   35% fat

Q | HOW DO I LOSE WEIGHT AND GAIN MUSCLE?
A | The common goals of most strength training programs are a reduction in body fat (which involves weight loss) combined with a gain in muscle mass (which involves weight gain). Neither a weight training nor a nutrition program on its own will have the desired effect, but in combination they will achieve the goal. Planning your training program without considering your diet will slow your progress, or even make you ill.

Q | HOW DO I ADD MUSCULAR BODYWEIGHT?
A | There's little to be gained by consuming large amounts of protein or protein supplements to build muscle because, depending on your weight and constitution, your body can absorb only $7/8$–$1\frac{1}{4}$oz (25–35g) of protein at one sitting. Stick to a balanced diet with frequent small meals (every 3–4 hours) and good natural protein sources from whole grains, beans and pulses, lean meat, fish, and eggs. This diet will give you all the protein you need for muscle growth.

Q | HOW DO I CONTROL FAT?
A | Fat is produced by your body when you take in more calories than you need to fuel body maintenance and support your current level of physical activity. There is some scientific evidence that we are genetically programmed to stay within roughly 26lb (12kg) of your optimal bodyweight.

Your body does not like change. It is programmed for "homeostasis"—maintaining its internal conditions at a steady level. This also applies to body weight; the more drastic the changes you try to impose, the more your body will fight against them. When you try to lose a large amount of weight over a short period, your body will respond by "slowing down"; your basic metabolic rate (BMR), which is the amount of energy that you use while at rest, will fall. This reduces performance in training and makes it harder to lose weight in the long run. You should limit weight loss to less than $2\frac{1}{4}$lb (1kg) per week.

Eating right: FAQs

Q | CAN I TARGET A SPECIFIC PART OF MY BODY FOR FAT LOSS?

A | You can't "spot reduce"—target fat loss to a particular part of the body. If you exercise a particular part of your body, the muscle tissue beneath the fat will become firmer and the appearance of that region will improve. However, the exercise may not specifically reduce fat in the area; fat deposits will diminish with appropriate nutrition and training wherever they are on the body. For instance, if you complete 300 abs crunches every day but maintain your fatty diet, you will develop strong abs, but they will be hidden under a layer of fat.

Q | WILL MY MUSCLE TURN TO FAT IF I STOP EXERCISING?

A | Muscle does not turn into fat and, conversely, no amount of exercise will turn fat into muscle. Muscle and fat are two are completely different types of tissue. When you stop a program of hard training yet you continue to eat in the way you did to fuel the exercise regimen, you are consequently taking in more calories than you are burning off and so a gain in body fat is absolutely inevitable. If you stop your healthy diet and start to eat junk then the problems get even worse and the fat builds up faster still.

Q | WHAT IS DIETARY FIBER?

A | Dietary fiber is also known as "roughage." It is the edible parts of plants that cannot be digested in the human intestines. Consuming enough fiber—around $5/8$oz (18g) per day for the average adult—is very important because adequate fiber helps prevent constipation and intestinal diseases. It also helps in lowering cholesterol levels and regulating blood sugar. Fiber is abundantly found in foods such as fruit, vegetables, beans, and whole-grain cereals.

Q | WHAT ARE HIGH AND LOW GI FOODS?

A | Low GI (glycemic index) foods release their energy slowly. They are an excellent basic fuel for sports—and for life—because they increase blood sugar levels slowly for ready use and so provide a boost of energy without the big "surge" that typifies high GI foods. High GI foods are very quickly absorbed and will typically give you a "sugar rush" or spike, followed by a trough when your energy levels drop below where they were before you ate. The result is that you may feel lethargic and sleepy—not a desirable feeling before or during a training session. You can replenish after your session by eating small quantities of high GI foods along with a little protein. Typical GI values for different foods are given below (see box, below).

GI SCORES

The GI of a food is given on a scale of 0–100, with 100 being pure sugar. Here are some examples of foods and their GIs :

Typical energy drink	95 GI
Cornflakes	80 GI
White bread	78 GI
Spaghetti (white)	61 GI
Ice cream	61 GI
Orange juice	52 GI
Whole-grain bread	51 GI
Spaghetti (wholemeal)	32 GI
Bran cereal	30 GI

A GI of 55 or less is considered low and 70+ high.

Q | HOW FREQUENTLY SHOULD I EAT EVERY DAY?

A | Always begin your day with a good breakfast of low GI foods then try to eat at three-hour intervals so that your body always has fuel to burn. Try not to skip meals; go for lower-calorie alternatives instead. Try snacking on fruits and yogurt and lean sources of protein. Skipping meals and feeling hungry puts the body on "red alert" and it starts to conserve fat.

Q | SHOULD I EAT ANYTHING SPECIAL AFTER MY WORKOUT?

A | If your training is recreational and of reasonable intensity and volume, the answer is "nothing special"; you should get everything you need from a healthy, balanced diet. However, if you are engaged in intense training with heavy weights, the period of 30 minutes after finishing is a crucial window of opportunity when you should take in high GI foods (about 50g/1¾oz) to replenish your glycogen stores. Combine this with protein to repair the tissues stressed during the workout.

Q | CAN I "SWEAT OFF" FAT IN THE SAUNA?

A | Unfortunately not. The little weight loss you experience in a sauna or steam room comes from losing water, not fat. The weight returns immediately after you consume fluid.

Q | WHAT IS GLYCOGEN?

A | Glycogen is one of the body's major fuel sources. It is basically the substance in which the body stores carbohydrates for the long term. The majority is stored in the muscles and the liver.

Q | ARE ALL DIETARY FATS CREATED EQUAL?

A | No. The type of fats you get from oily fish (Omega 3 fats) are important in a healthy diet. Saturated fats, which are found in foods like whole milk and in the skin of grilled chicken, are best avoided as far as possible.

Q | DOES THE RIGHT MIX OF VITAMINS AND MINERALS MATTER FOR FUNCTIONING OF A HEALTHY BODY?

A | Yes. A lack of minerals can cause serious problems. At one end of the scale, you may experience muscular cramps after severe sweating. In the most serious cases mineral deficiency combined with dehydration can cause heart malfunction and even death. Vitamins are crucial to the chemical processes on which the healthy body depends. Some vitamins are fat soluble and so require some fat in the diet if they are to be absorbed.

Q | WHAT IS THE DIFFERENCE BETWEEN "ESSENTIAL FAT" AND "STORAGE FAT"?

A | There are two types of body fat. Essential fat is needed for normal body function, especially of the hormone and immune systems. It is present in the heart, lungs, spleen, kidneys, and other organs. Women carry more essential fat than men. This gender-specific fat is important for child bearing and other hormone-related functions. Storage fat is the fat that you lose or put on as your weight changes; it is laid down by your body in various areas, especially your hips, thighs, and abdomen in times of plenty, to be used in times of need.

" MUSCLE DOES NOT TURN INTO FAT AND NO AMOUNT OF EXERCISE WILL TURN FAT INTO MUSCLE. **"**

The Warm-up

Neck extension and flexion

This easy movement, which can be carried out standing or seated, will help prevent general neck stiffness. It will also give you an advantage in sports in which head position and movement are important—for example, where you need to follow a fast-moving ball or other object.

❝ THIS MOVEMENT **PREVENTS NECK STIFFNESS** AND CAN GIVE YOU AN ADVANTAGE IN CERTAIN SPORTS. ❞

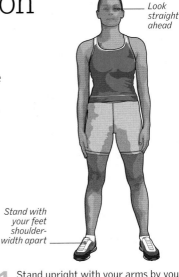

Look straight ahead

Stand with your feet shoulder-width apart

1 Stand upright with your arms by your sides in a relaxed posture or clasp your hands together to prevent your shoulders from rising. Look straight ahead and keep your spine in a neutral position.

Neck rotation

This very simple movement can help ease neck aches. It helps to maintain neck flexibility and delays or prevents age-related stiffening. You should be able to rotate your neck through at least 70 degrees to each side without feeling "pulls" or hearing cracking sounds.

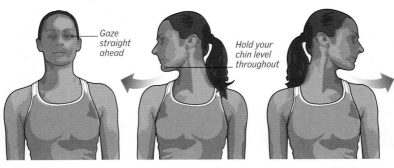

Gaze straight ahead

Hold your chin level throughout

1 Begin by looking straight ahead, holding your spine in a neutral position. Keep your upper body relaxed and your arms loose by your sides.

2 Move your head slowly to the side to look over your right shoulder. Turn as far as you can comfortably go, then hold for a few seconds.

3 Move your head back through the midline, until you are looking over your left shoulder, without straining. Return to the start position.

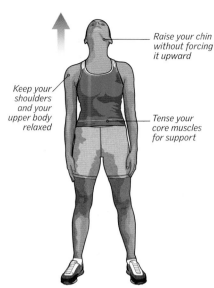

Raise your chin without forcing it upward

Keep your shoulders and your upper body relaxed

Tense your core muscles for support

2 Extend your neck by slowly raising your chin so you are looking up at the ceiling. Hold for a few seconds. Do not force the movement beyond a position that feels comfortable.

3 Flex your neck by letting your head drop forward without straining. Return your head to the start position and repeat the process slowly and with a gentle rhythm.

Neck side flexion

Imbalances in the muscles of the neck and shoulders can arise from a poor sleeping position or bad posture; they may cause pain or headaches, especially in sedentary office workers. This exercise is ideal for those with aching muscles in the upper back and neck.

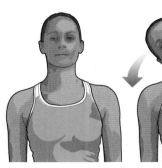

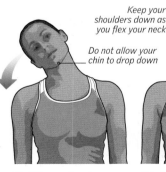

Keep your shoulders down as you flex your neck

Do not allow your chin to drop down

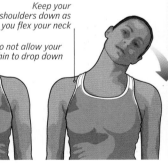

1 Stand upright, holding your body in a relaxed posture, with your shoulders loose and your eyes looking straight ahead.

2 Tilt your head so that your right ear moves toward your right shoulder. Tilt your head as far as it is comfortable. Hold this position for a few seconds.

3 Flex your neck in the opposite direction, passing through the start position, to the limit of flexion. Hold and return to step 1.

Arm circle

Many strength training exercises involve your arms and shoulders, so it makes good sense to warm them up thoroughly. Get your blood flowing, your muscles warmed up, and your joints moving fluently by circling your arms in a continuous smooth motion.

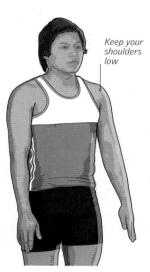

Keep your shoulders low

Keep your chest high

Contract your abs

1 Let your arms hang loose by your sides. Keep your shoulders down and relaxed. Look straight ahead and maintain a neutral spine.

2 Raise both arms to the front and start to make wide circles. Breathe easily and do not arch your spine.

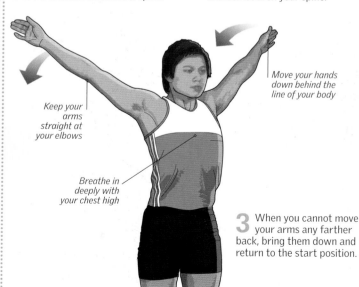

Move your hands down behind the line of your body

Keep your arms straight at your elbows

Breathe in deeply with your chest high

3 When you cannot move your arms any farther back, bring them down and return to the start position.

Shoulder rotation

The stability of your shoulder joints comes from the muscles and ligaments around them, rather than from your skeletal system. This exercise provides an excellent way of freeing up your shoulder joints, and also warming your trapezius muscles, before beginning a resistance training session.

> THIS EXERCISE **FREES UP YOUR SHOULDER JOINTS**, AND **WARMS UP THE TRAPEZIUS MUSCLES**, BEFORE YOU START A RESISTANCE TRAINING SESSION.

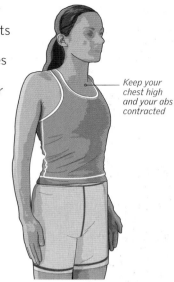

Keep your chest high and your abs contracted

1 Let your arms hang loose by your sides and keep your shoulders relaxed. Keep your head level and your spine in a neutral position.

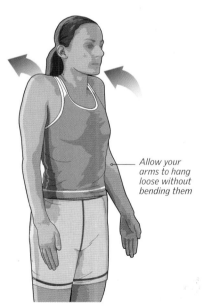

Allow your arms to hang loose without bending them

2 Bring your shoulders forward and inward and raise them slowly up toward your ears.

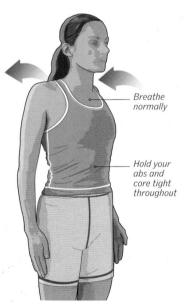

Breathe normally

Hold your abs and core tight throughout

3 Rotate your shoulders to the rear and then back to the start position, still looking straight ahead.

Wrist rotation

A good grip is fundamental to performing many upper body exercises. Wrist rotation helps ensure that your wrist joints are mobile and ready for work. It also helps to prevent wrist injuries like carpal tunnel syndrome that commonly affect desk workers.

Keep your wrists loose and relaxed

Hold your body firmly and your spine neutral

1 Hold your arms out to either side, level with your shoulders.

Ensure that your shoulders remain in the same plane

Use your abs and core to hold your body solidly

2 Make small circles with your hands around your wrist joints. Move slowly, rolling your wrists, rather than moving them from side to side.

Move your wrist through all its natural positions

3 Continue the rolling action for around 20 seconds before reversing the direction of rotation of your hands.

Hip circle

The core muscles of your torso are involved in many strength training movements, especially those performed standing up. This exercise, in which you rotate your hips as if swinging a hula-hoop around your body, helps to mobilize your core muscles.

Take up a relaxed posture

Keep your legs straight throughout

Ensure that you circle your hips only

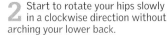

1 Stand upright with your hands on your hips, your legs straight, and your feet shoulder-width—or slightly more—apart.

2 Start to rotate your hips slowly in a clockwise direction without arching your lower back.

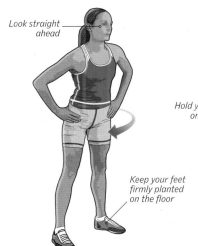

Look straight ahead

Keep your feet firmly planted on the floor

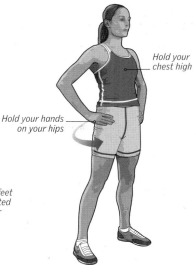

Hold your chest high

Hold your hands on your hips

3 Continue the rotation. Do not jerk your body into position; smooth movement is essential throughout.

4 After 10–15 repetitions, return to the start position and reverse your direction, rotating counterclockwise.

Torso rotation

This exercise complements the hip circle (see p.41) in mobilizing your core muscles, but here your upper body moves while your hips remain stationary.

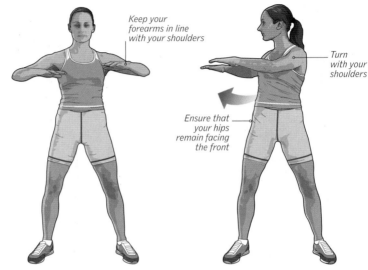

Keep your forearms in line with your shoulders

Turn with your shoulders

Ensure that your hips remain facing the front

1 Stand upright, with your feet shoulder-width apart and elbows raised to each side.

2 Rotate your upper body smoothly to your right, keeping your elbows and forearms in line.

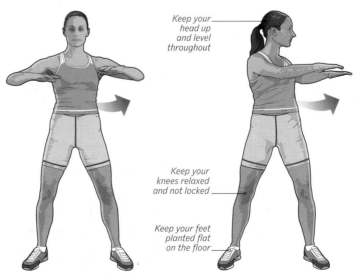

Keep your head up and level throughout

Keep your knees relaxed and not locked

Keep your feet planted flat on the floor

3 Rotate back through the start position, keeping your movement fluid, not jerky.

4 Continue the rotation to your left, keeping your elbows up. Return to the start position.

Trunk flexion

After performing the hip circle (see p.41) and torso rotation (see opposite), mobilize your upper body by flexing from side to side. This engages your core muscles at a different angle.

Keep your feet planted on the floor

1 Stand upright, with your arms by your sides and close to your body. Keep your shoulders relaxed.

Move only your upper body

2 Flex your upper body sideways, sliding your left hand down your leg as far as it will go. Don't lean forward or back and don't "bounce" at the end of the movement.

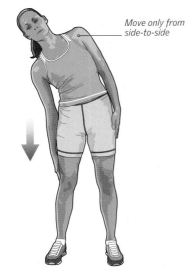

Move only from side-to-side

3 Repeat for your right-hand side, taking your hand down as far as it will go. Return to the start position.

“MOBILIZE YOUR UPPER BODY BY FLEXING FROM SIDE TO SIDE. THIS ENGAGES YOUR CORE MUSCLES AT A DIFFERENT ANGLE.”

Frankenstein walk

This exercise mobilizes your hips and hamstrings. You can perform it standing in one spot or walking. It is important to keep a steady tempo and extend your front leg under tight control rather than swinging too enthusiastically.

> ❝ THIS EXERCISE MOBILIZES YOUR **HAMSTRINGS AND HIPS**. ❞

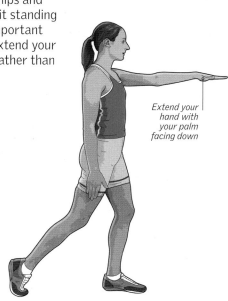

Extend your hand with your palm facing down

1 Start from a standing position. Keep your body upright, with your right leg slightly behind the line of your body, resting on your toe; hold your left arm horizontally in front of your body.

Do not drop your front arm down toward your foot

Keep your rear foot flat on the floor

Point your toes up

Keep your rear leg straight and solid

2 Resting securely on your left leg, kick your right leg up, while keeping your knee as straight as possible.

3 Bring your front leg up to touch your hand (or as near as your flexibility will allow). Recover and repeat with your other leg.

Pike walk

This challenging mobilizer works your calves, hamstrings, and the core muscles of your lower back. With practice, some people can bend almost in half, but persevere if your movement is more limited.

1 Position yourself as if you were about to perform a push-up, with your hands shoulder-width apart and flat on the floor, and your arms straight.

Keep your spine in a neutral position

Support your weight on your toes

Maintain a straight line through your hips

2 "Walk" your hands into a position in front of your head. Then keeping your legs straight, slowly walk your feet up toward your hands.

Fold your body at your hips

Keep your core and abs tight

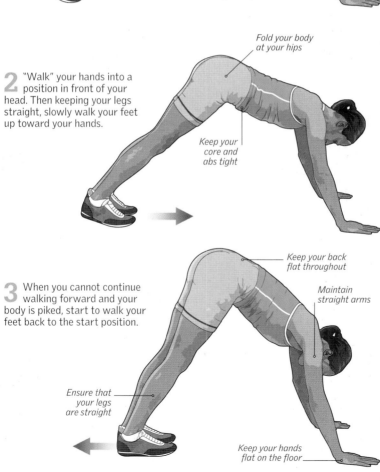

3 When you cannot continue walking forward and your body is piked, start to walk your feet back to the start position.

Keep your back flat throughout

Maintain straight arms

Ensure that your legs are straight

Keep your hands flat on the floor

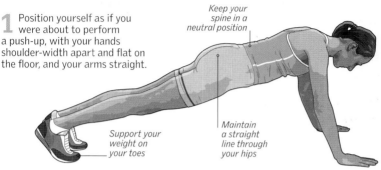

Leg flexion

This mobilizer targets your hips and hamstrings. Like the more difficult Frankenstein walk (see p.44), this exercise involves moving one leg at a time; however, here both your moving leg and your stabilizing limb are worked at once.

Keep your trailing leg as straight as possible

Tense and hold your core muscles for support

Bend your knee very slightly for balance

1 Stand on your left leg with your right leg slightly behind the line of your body. Rest your right foot on tiptoe. Place your left palm against a wall for balance.

2 Keep your left foot firm and flat on the floor, and raise your right leg, stretching it out in front of you. Keep your right knee as straight as possible.

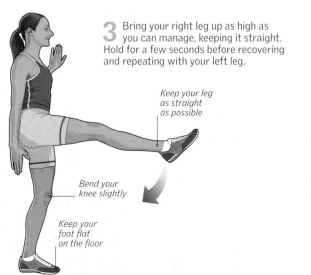

3 Bring your right leg up as high as you can manage, keeping it straight. Hold for a few seconds before recovering and repeating with your left leg.

Keep your leg as straight as possible

Bend your knee slightly

Keep your foot flat on the floor

Leg abduction

In this hip mobilizer you move your leg in a different arc from that in the leg flexion (see opposite). It works to free up your glutes and the muscles in your groin area.

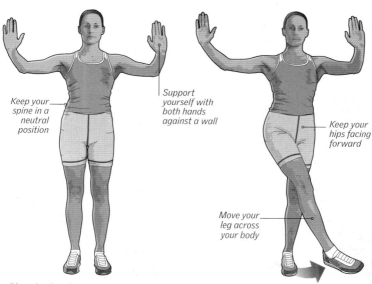

Keep your spine in a neutral position

Support yourself with both hands against a wall

Keep your hips facing forward

Move your leg across your body

1 Place both palms against a wall with your body leaning slightly forward. Shift your weight on to your left leg.

2 In a controlled manner, swing your right leg across your body, pointing your toes out at the end of the swing.

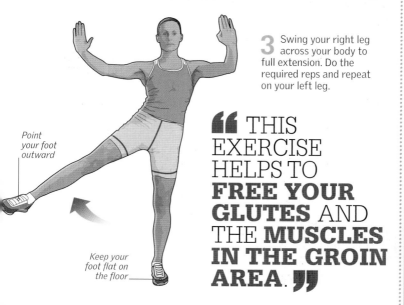

3 Swing your right leg across your body to full extension. Do the required reps and repeat on your left leg.

Point your foot outward

Keep your foot flat on the floor

❝ THIS EXERCISE HELPS TO FREE YOUR GLUTES AND THE MUSCLES IN THE GROIN AREA. ❞

Lunge

This is an excellent way to mobilize your hips and thighs. You can perform the exercise either in one fixed position (like a split squat, see pp.116–17) or with alternate legs, stepping forward. The lunge tests both your balance and coordination, making it an excellent mobility exercise for all sports.

Keep your legs straight

1 Begin upright with your feet shoulder-width apart, arms relaxed by your sides, feet flat on the floor, chest high, and spine neutral.

Hold your shoulders shrugged back

Engage your core muscles for stability

Keep your back leg straight

Put your weight on the heel of your front foot

2 Breathe in and take a stride forward so that your front foot is flat on the ground, your front leg flexed, your body upright, and your head facing forward.

Maintain an upright torso and a neutral spine

Extend your knee above your toes

Do not touch the floor with your rear knee

> ❝ THIS EXERCISE **MOBILIZES YOUR HIPS AND THIGHS** AND TESTS YOUR BALANCE. ❞

3 Bend your front and back legs so that your rear knee drops close to the floor. Push back up with your front heel and return to the standing position.

Rotational lunge

This is a good mobilizer for your hips and thighs. You should feel it stretch the hip flexor of your back leg and the glute of your front leg. It also engages your torso.

Bring your arm across your body

Extend your right arm out; keep it parallel to the floor

Rotate your whole torso

Raise your back heel from the floor

1 Follow steps 1 and 2 as for the lunge (see opposite), but as you descend, start to turn your torso to the right at your waist. Turn your head, extend the opposite arm across your body, and twist.

Overhead lunge

This more demanding version of the lunge movement mobilizes your hips and thighs. Adding a light weight overhead works the stabilizers in your shoulders and puts emphasis on the mobility of your hips and lower back.

1 Adopt the lunge start position (see opposite) while holding a light bar over your head with your hands widely spaced.

2 Take the lunge step with your right leg, holding the bar over your center of gravity, which falls between your legs. Return to the start position and repeat on your left leg.

Engage your core muscles

Hold the bar with your arms straight above your shoulders

Keep your chest high and your shoulders back

Lift your heel off the floor

Exercises

Push-up

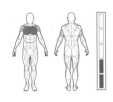

This is one of the simplest but most effective exercises for your chest, shoulders, and arms. Its added benefit is that it requires no apparatus—just your own body weight.

1 Support your body on your toes with your arms straight, positioned under, and just a little wider than your shoulders. Breathe in and lower your body slowly and under control until your torso just touches the floor.

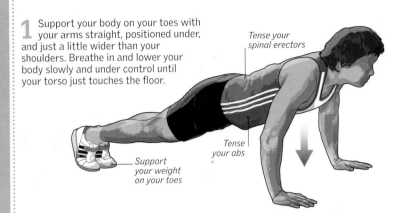

Tense your spinal erectors

Tense your abs

Support your weight on your toes

2 Hold the bottom position for a second, then breathe out and push your torso up until your arms are straight and you are back to the start position. Keep the angle of your back constant and your head forward.

Maintain a neutral spine

Keep your legs straight

Point your fingers forward

Do not allow your trunk to sag

VARIATION

To engage the stabilizers of your torso more than in the regular push-up, try using a stability ball. Place your hands on the ball and lower your body to the point where your arms are bent at a 90-degree angle and press back up.

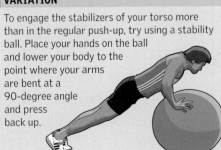

66 THIS IS ONE OF THE MOST EFFECTIVE EXERCISES FOR YOUR **CHEST**, **SHOULDERS**, **AND ARMS**. 99

Frame-supported push-up

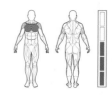

Using a pair of frames will give you a greater range of motion than with the standard push-up (see opposite).

1 Place the frames wider than shoulder-width apart. Hold your body straight, resting on your toes and straightened arms. Breathe in and lower your body until the line of the body is below your flexed elbows.

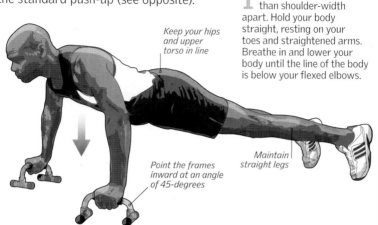

Keep your hips and upper torso in line

Point the frames inward at an angle of 45-degrees

Maintain straight legs

2 Pause for a second at the bottom of the motion. Press back up until you return to the start position.

Keep your torso tight

Support your weight on your toes

WARNING

Do not let your torso sag as you push yourself up. This will cut down the range of your movement, diminishing the effect on your chest, shoulders, and arms. Failure to straighten your arms after each rep will also make the exercise less effective.

VARIATION

Increase the challenge by placing your feet on a bench. The higher your feet, the more your shoulders are brought into play. You can move the frames wider or closer. Close spacing will work your triceps more.

Chest

Machine bench press

This is a good chest exercise for beginners or those nervous about working with free weights. Be sure to adjust the machine to match your height and limb length.

Adjust the grip width to suit your build

1 Set your desired weight on the stack. Take an overhand grip on the handles, which should be at midchest level.

Keep your feet flat on the floor

Press on the handles and extend your arms

2 Breathe in deeply, then breathe out as you press the handles in a slow and controlled movement; keep your body tight against the pads.

3 Fully extend your arms, then return the handles to the start position, breathing in. Don't let the weight rest on the stack before starting another rep.

Machine fly

This can be a useful companion exercise to the machine bench press (see opposite). It allows you to work your chest muscles through a greater range of motion while keeping your body well supported.

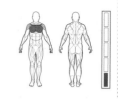

The handles of the machine swivel, taking pressure off your wrists

1 Set your desired weight on the stack. Allow your arms to spread in a wide arc so that the handles are just behind the line of your torso.

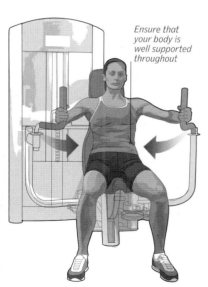

Ensure that your body is well supported throughout

2 Breathe out, bringing the handles together in a wide arc, with your elbows slightly bent. This is similar to a hugging motion.

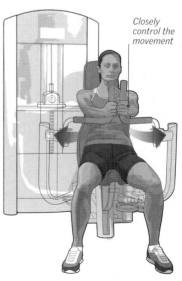

Closely control the movement

3 When the movement is complete and your knuckles touch, contract your chest muscles and begin the return phase, back to the start position.

Chest

Cable cross-over

In this chest and shoulder exercise, your body is not supported by a bench, so the stabilizing muscles of your core and legs have to work to keep you in position. Using the cable machine also works your muscles over a large range of motion.

1 Set the pulley to its highest position and select your desired weight on the stack. Leaning slightly forward and with your legs braced, bring the pulley handles down across your body. Breathe in and let your arms travel back in a wide arc so that they are just behind the line of your torso. This is the start position.

Keep your head still and your eyes forward

Keep your elbows slightly unlocked

Maintain a neutral spine

Place one foot forward and one back for balance

2 Bring your arms down and across your body in a wide arc—like a hugging motion. Keep your head up and maintain a slight bend in your arms as you pull the handles forward and down at a slight angle. Breathe out on the effort.

Ensure that your palms face in

Slightly bend your front knee

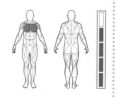

USING **THE CABLE MACHINE** WORKS YOUR MUSCLES OVER A **LARGE RANGE OF MOTION**.

WARNING

Choose a weight that is not so heavy as to pull your body back from its braced position. Do not use the momentum of your body to complete the movement because you will almost certainly lose balance and risk injury.

3 Bring your hands to the front of your body before starting the return phase, reversing the arc of movement in Step 2. Make sure that your arms move at the same speed and that your elbows stay in the same slightly bent position throughout the movement.

Control the momentum of your body

Bring the cables together; you can cross them over at the center point

VARIATION

You can also perform the cable cross-over exercise at varying heights. Set the pulley to a low position or to waist height. Ensure that the height of the pulley allows a comfortable movement. These different start positions allow you to work your chest muscles from slightly different angles.

Barbell bench press

This classic chest exercise is a great motivator. It offers huge potential for increasing strength and most people can progress rapidly to heavier weights.

1 Lift the bar from the rack and hold it over your chest at shoulder-length distance. Make sure your head, shoulders, and buttocks are pressed solidly on the bench.

Wrap your thumbs around the bar

2 Breathe in and lower the bar to your midchest area. Lower your arms together until your forearms are vertical at the low point.

Lower the bar in a shallow arc

Hold your chest high

3 Push the bar upward, following the same arc in which you lowered it. Finish each rep over your chest with straight arms.

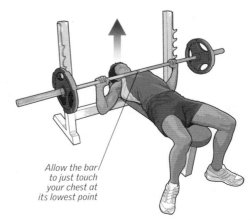

Allow the bar to just touch your chest at its lowest point

Dumbbell bench press

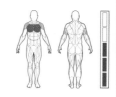

Working the main muscles of your chest, the dumbbell bench press gives an increased range of movement over a barbell (see opposite), so can boost muscle growth even further.

> **THE DUMBELL BENCH PRESS GIVES AN INCREASED RANGE OF MOVEMENT OVER A BARBELL.**

1 Raise the dumbells over your collarbones. Keep your shoulders, head, and hips pressed against the bench.

Lower the weights under control

Keep your forearms vertical under the weights

2 Lower the weights together slowly and under control, keeping them aligned across the middle of your chest.

Lift the weights in a shallow arc

3 Press the weights back up in a shallow arc until they are together above your chest once again.

Chest

Incline barbell bench press

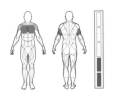

This is one of the basic movements for developing your chest. You will be able to lift less at an incline than flat because the smaller muscles of your shoulders come into play.

> **❝ PERFORMING THIS EXERCISE ON AN INCLINE** UTILIZES THE **SMALLER MUSCLES** IN YOUR **SHOULDERS**. ❞

1 Grip the bar securely with your hands more than shoulder-width apart. Place your feet flat on the floor and lift the bar from the rack.

Hold your chest high

Secure the weights on the bar with collars

Brace your feet firmly against the floor

2 Lower the bar to the top of your chest so that your forearms are nearly vertical under the bar. Press your shoulders against the bench.

3 Keeping your head pressed against the bench and your spine neutral, straighten your arms evenly until the bar reaches the start position.

Chest

Incline dumbbell bench press

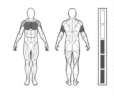

Similar to the incline barbell press (see opposite), this exercise allows a greater range of motion and so is of even greater value in functional terms for sports training purposes.

WARNING

Make sure that you raise and lower the weights evenly. Avoid jerking or twisting your body to "muscle" them upward. Keep your body well balanced by holding the weights directly over your shoulders at the start.

Extend your arms straight over your shoulders

1 Lift the dumbbells over your shoulder joints on straight arms. The dumbbells should touch at the top of the movement.

Keep your head, shoulders, and buttocks well supported

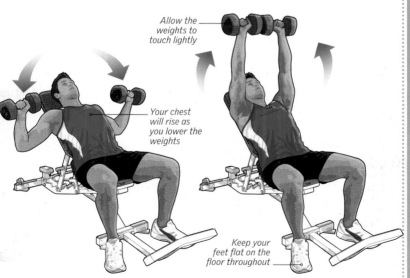

Allow the weights to touch lightly

Your chest will rise as you lower the weights

Keep your feet flat on the floor throughout

2 Lower the dumbbells slowly and evenly to the point at which your upper arms are near vertical and the weights are level with your shoulders.

3 Push the weights upward in a shallow arc back to the start position. Fully extend your arms and let the dumbbells touch lightly.

Chest

Incline fly

This popular dumbbell chest exercise also helps develop your shoulders. An excellent companion exercise to the incline press (see p.60), it offers you a greater range of motion to work the large muscles of your chest.

WARNING

Ensure that you do not overdo the weight—this could lead to poor form and the risk of injury. Using heavy weights also means that you are likely to engage your triceps over your chest muscles.

1 Set the bench at a 45-degree angle. With your palms facing in, lift the dumbbells to arm's length above your shoulders so that they just touch. Ensure that your hips and back are well supported on the bench.

Hold the dumbbells so that they just touch

Slightly unlock your elbows

Ensure that your lower back is well supported

Brace your feet against the floor

Maintain a constant angle at your elbows

Feel a stretch in your chest

2 Breathe in deeply and bring the dumbbells down slowly and under control in a wide arc. Do not let the dumbbells drop vertically or allow your arms to twist.

Chest

VARIATION

The fly may also be done on a flat bench. Begin with the same dumbbell position as for the incline fly and use the same arm-hugging motion to bring the dumbbells together in a shallow arc.

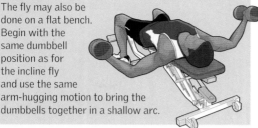

Move the dumbbells up in same arc as in descent

Move your arms in a "hugging" action

Keep your elbows slightly bent

3 Finish the movement when the dumbbells are level with your ears and begin the return phase, breathing out as you go.

Bring the weights together gently

4 Return to the start position, bringing the weights together over your body slowly and under control.

Keep your feet braced against the floor throughout

Chin-up

One of the most effective strength builders for the back, this exercise is ideal in training for sports that involve gripping and grappling. When starting out, begin with the assisted version (see p.70) to build strength and promote muscular development.

Take a neutral grip with medium hand spacing

Hang on fully extended arms

1 Select the desired hand spacing and drop down on fully extended arms. Bend your knees and cross your feet to improve your stability.

Pull your body up

2 From a hanging position, flex at your elbows and shoulders, and start to pull your body up. Don't swing your legs or bend at the hips to gain extra momentum.

Lift your chin above your hands

3 Continue to pull your body upward vertically until your chin passes the level of your hands. Keep your shoulders back.

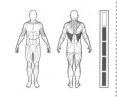

Keep your chest pushed forward

THIS STRENGTH BUILDER FOR THE BACK IS IDEAL IN TRAINING FOR SPORTS THAT INVOLVE **GRIPPING AND GRAPPLING**.

4 Pause at the top of the movement, then begin to lower your body slowly and under control. Look ahead, not down to the floor.

5 Return to the start position with your legs in line with your torso and your arms fully extended—don't cheat by stopping short on your descent.

VARIATION

Try varying your grip and hand spacing. An overhand grip uses your biceps less, so is tougher than an underhand grip. A narrow grip hits the smaller muscles in your shoulders, while a wide grip is more challenging on your lats, although it stresses your elbows.

Back extension

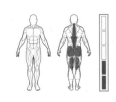

This is a great core exercise in which you flex your body around your hip joints while keeping your spine neutral. Your hamstring flexibility will determine the degree of flexion you can achieve.

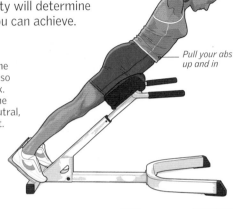

1 Position your thighs on the pads of the Roman chair so that your hips are free to flex. Your feet should be flat on the foot supports, your spine neutral, and your elbows pointing out.

Pull your abs up and in

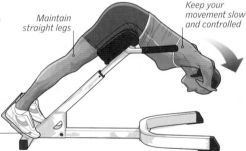

2 Flex at your hips and drop your upper body toward the floor. Keep your back flat. Stop bending when flexibility of your hamstrings restricts further movement.

Maintain straight legs

Keep your movement slow and controlled

Keep your feet flat on the support

3 Return to the start position, contracting your hamstrings, glutes, and spinal erectors. Do not extend beyond the start position as you may injure your back.

Do not extend back beyond the start position

Seated pulley row

This is a key muscle builder and strength developer for your back. However, good technique is important if you are to achieve optimum results safely.

1 Select the desired resistance from the stack. Push with your legs until your arms are fully extended and your back is in a neutral position. Bend your knees to an angle of around 90 degrees.

Begin with straight arms

Bend at the knees

2 Draw your elbows back, maintaining a neutral spine position and an upright body. Keep your feet braced flat against the foot rests of the rowing machine.

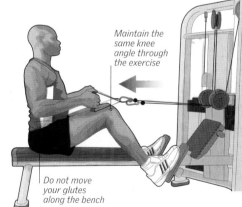

Maintain the same knee angle through the exercise

Do not move your glutes along the bench

3 Pull the handles toward your body at the level of your upper abdomen. Exhale and draw your elbows back as far as possible. When you return to the start position, inhale and straighten your arms in a controlled manner. Don't let the weight pull you in toward the stack.

Keep your back at a 90-degree angle to the bench

Back

Standing pulley row

This exercise will help you achieve great results in terms of your back strength and development, with minimal risk of injury.

1 Set the pulley low and select your desired weight on the stack. Stand up with the weight and lower your body into a shallow squat.

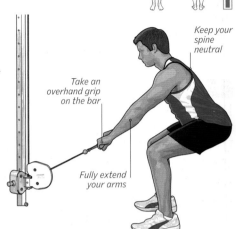

Take an overhand grip on the bar

Keep your spine neutral

Fully extend your arms

2 Maintain the shallow squat position, ensuring that your back stays flat. Pull the bar toward you, aiming for your upper abdomen.

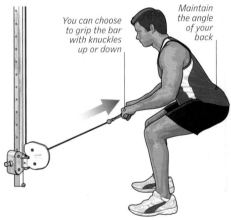

You can choose to grip the bar with knuckles up or down

Maintain the angle of your back

3 Pull the bar all the way into your body. Pause, then return to the start position with straight arms, slowly and under full control.

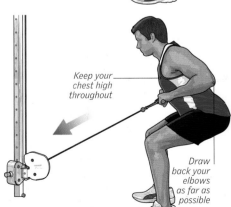

Keep your chest high throughout

Draw back your elbows as far as possible

Lat pull-down

This is another good exercise for your back if you lack the upper body strength to lift your own bodyweight in the regular chin-up (see p.64). You can increase the resistance to build strength gradually.

❝❝ THIS EXERCISE DEVELOPS THE MUSCLES IN YOUR UPPER BODY. INCREASE RESISTANCE GRADUALLY TO BUILD STRENGTH. ❞❞

Keep your body upright under the pulley and your arms straight

1 Select the desired resistance on the stack. Grip the bar a little wider than shoulder-width, then sit down and place your upper thighs under the pad.

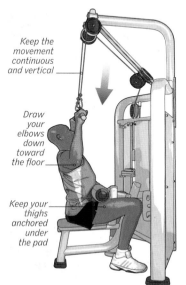

Keep the movement continuous and vertical

Draw your elbows down toward the floor

Keep your thighs anchored under the pad

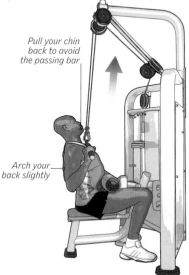

Pull your chin back to avoid the passing bar

Arch your back slightly

2 Easing your body back slightly, pull the bar down to the top of your chest. Make sure your elbows are drawn in to your upper body as far as possible.

3 Once the bar touches the upper part of your chest, allow it to return slowly and under full control until your arms are completely extended.

Assisted chin-up

This is a great way to work your big back muscles and practice the movement of the regular chin-up (see p.64) if you lack the strength to lift your whole body weight. Remember that adding weight to the stack makes the exercise easier.

1 Select the weight from the stack; and stand on the foot rests. Choose your grip (see p.65) and place one knee then the other on the pad, and ensure your arms are straight.

Kneel on the pad

Hold your feet together

Choose a suitable grip width

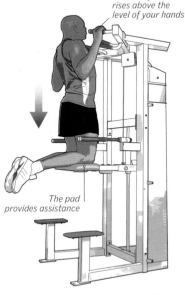

Pull until your chin rises above the level of your hands

The pad provides assistance

2 Bend at your elbows and shoulders and use your lats to pull your body up. Keep your body straight; breathe out going up and in going down.

3 Pull your body up until your chin is above the line of the hand grips. Pause, then lower your body by reversing the movement till your arms are straight.

Straight-arm pull-down

This important upper back exercise uses the stabilizers of your core, your quads, and your glutes to fix you in position. Avoid this exercise if you suffer from any shoulder problems.

1 Set the pulley high and select your desired weight. Hold a straight bar in an overhand grip. Brace your legs and glutes.

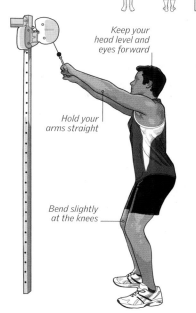

Keep your head level and eyes forward

Hold your arms straight

Bend slightly at the knees

Maintain straight arms throughout the movement

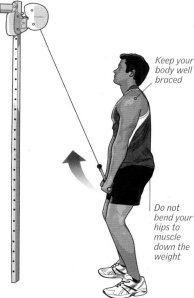

Keep your body well braced

Do not bend your hips to muscle down the weight

2 Bring the bar down slowly in a controlled movement. Do not lean forward or allow your weight to shift forward into the movement.

3 Bring the bar all the way down to your upper thighs in an arc. Pause, then return slowly to the start position following the same arc.

Back

Prone row

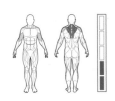

This twist on the dumbbell row is great for developing your upper back and strengthening your core. You could try it on an exercise ball rather than a bench to further work your stabilizers.

Support your feet on the apparatus

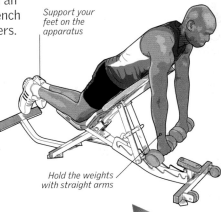

1 Position your body on an incline bench at a 45-degree angle. Hold the dumbbells in an overhand grip and lie chest-down against the pad.

Hold the weights with straight arms

2 Bending your elbows, pull your upper arms back as high as is comfortable, while keeping them at right angles to your torso. Squeeze together your shoulder blades at the end of the movement.

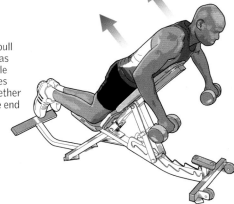

3 Pause briefly at the top of the movement, then lower the weights slowly and under control to the start position.

Keep your elbows in line with your wrists

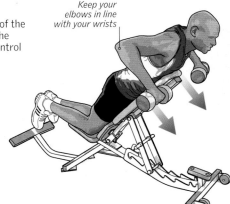

WARNING

Keep your hips pressed into the bench and do not lift or turn your head, or flex your neck. Your torso and legs should remain in one position throughout.

One-arm row

This is an easy exercise to get great
results in back strength and development,
with minimal risk of injury.

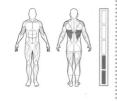

**❝ THIS EXERCISE
OFFERS GREAT
RESULTS IN BACK
STRENGTH AND
DEVELOPMENT. ❞**

1 Rest one knee on a
bench. Holding your
back flat, brace your
body with your free
arm. Hold the dumbbell
with one hand.

*Hold the dumbbell
with your arm straight*

2 Hold your back flat
and your shoulders
level. Raise the dumbbell
toward your body with
your elbow pointing up.

*Keep your back flat
and well supported*

*Keep your head steady,
and your eyes looking
forward and slightly down*

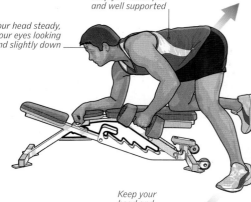

3 Pull your elbow
as high as possible
before returning, under
control, to the start
position. Complete one
set, then repeat with
your other arm.

*Keep your
head and
hips in line*

*Support
part of your
body weight
on your arm*

Back

Bent-over row

This is one of the most important exercises for the large muscles of your back—the latissimus dorsi—and will give you the classic "V" shape. It is a multijoint exercise that builds good posture, helps prevent back injuries, and also provides a thorough lower-body and core workout.

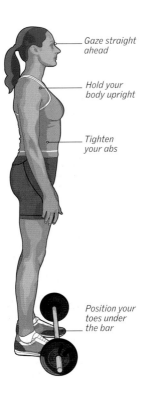

Gaze straight ahead

Hold your body upright

Tighten your abs

1 Stand upright with your head level, your core muscles engaged, and your toes under the bar. Shrug your shoulders back and slightly down, hollowing your back.

Position your toes under the bar

Keep your back flat

4 Partially straighten your legs, and keep the angle of your back constant until the bar is just below your knees. Your body should feel stable and braced at your hips.

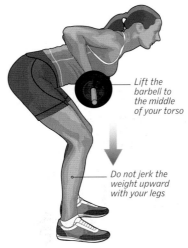

Lift the barbell to the middle of your torso

Do not jerk the weight upward with your legs

5 Bring the barbell up, flexing your arms and raising your elbows until they touch your body. Pause, then let your elbows extend back to the start position (Step 3) and repeat.

2 Bending your knees over the bar, lower your body, keeping your spine neutral. Keep your feet shoulder-width apart and look straight ahead.

Maintain a neutral spine

3 Grasp the bar in an overhand grip with your arms outside your knees. Keep your back flat, your heels pressed down on the floor, and your head forward.

Move your shoulders over the bar

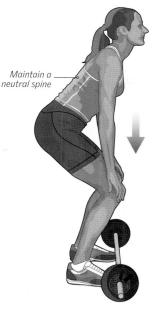

❝ THIS EXERCISE **BUILDS GOOD POSTURE** AND GIVES YOU THE **CLASSIC 'V' SHAPE**. ❞

Keep your back tight throughout

Flex your hips to lower your body

6 At the end of your set, lower the barbell to the ground by bending your knees, keeping your back at a constant angle. Don't swing the weight at any point in the exercise.

WARNING

Keep your back straight; if you allow it to become rounded and lose its flat, neutral position, the forces acting on the base of your spine increase dramatically and the risk of injury becomes high. Do not allow your shoulders to collapse forward during or after the lift when you return the bar to the floor.

Barbell pull-over

This is an excellent exercise to develop the size of your chest and improve the overall posture of your upper body, and is a useful exercise if you are training for throwing sports or martial arts. However, you should avoid it if you have any shoulder problems.

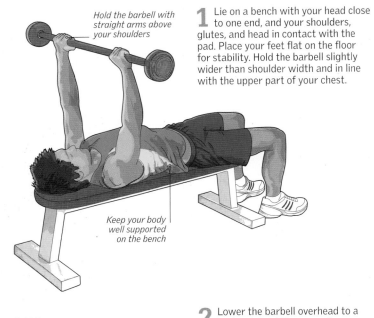

Hold the barbell with straight arms above your shoulders

1 Lie on a bench with your head close to one end, and your shoulders, glutes, and head in contact with the pad. Place your feet flat on the floor for stability. Hold the barbell slightly wider than shoulder width and in line with the upper part of your chest.

Keep your body well supported on the bench

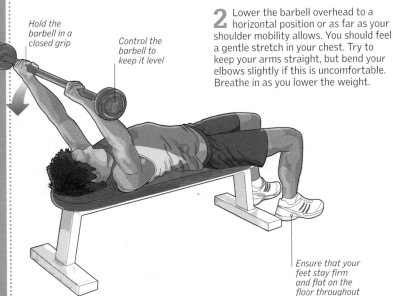

Hold the barbell in a closed grip

Control the barbell to keep it level

2 Lower the barbell overhead to a horizontal position or as far as your shoulder mobility allows. You should feel a gentle stretch in your chest. Try to keep your arms straight, but bend your elbows slightly if this is uncomfortable. Breathe in as you lower the weight.

Ensure that your feet stay firm and flat on the floor throughout

VARIATION

You can perform this exercise with a narrow grip on the barbell, using an EZ bar, or with a single dumbbell. In all these variations you can bend your arms slightly on the downward movement past the head. This allows a greater range of movement and puts more emphasis on the triceps. In each case, ensure that your feet stay planted on the floor.

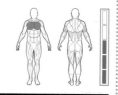

WARNING

Using excessive weight can cause your lower back to arch and damage your intervertebral disks. Use a weight light enough to help maintain good form through the full range of movement.

Do not allow the barbell to drop below the level of your torso

Keep your lower back and hips against the bench

3 Pause momentarily at the extreme of the movement, then keeping your arms straight, raise the barbell to the upright position. Breathe out as you do so.

Hold the bar over the middle of your chest

Try not to bend your arms to help with the load

4 Back at the start position, take a little time to check your body alignment and foot placement before starting on the next repetition.

Bench dip

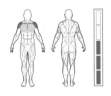

Bench dips are a good general upper-body exercise and ideal training for the bench press. You can perform this exercise using just one bench to support your arms, though a second, lower bench beneath your feet makes the movement easier.

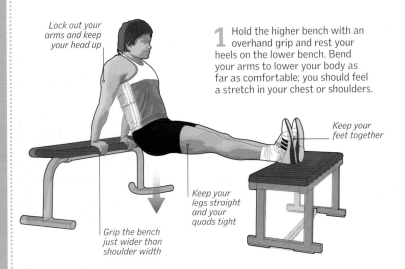

Lock out your arms and keep your head up

1 Hold the higher bench with an overhand grip and rest your heels on the lower bench. Bend your arms to lower your body as far as comfortable; you should feel a stretch in your chest or shoulders.

Keep your feet together

Keep your legs straight and your quads tight

Grip the bench just wider than shoulder width

Bend your arms to an angle of 90 degrees

2 Your shoulder mobility will determine how low you can go. At the lowest point, extend your arms and return to the start under control.

Feel your hamstrings tighten

WARNING

Make sure that the benches or other supports you use are strong and stable enough to carry your weight and that they are of sufficient height to allow you a full range of motion.

Do not force your shoulder joints beyond their normal range of movement and keep from rounding your back or allowing it to move away too far from the edge of the bench.

Arms

Bar dip

Bar dips help to build upper-body strength and are ideal in training for throwing events. Good technique takes practice; if you are just starting out, let the knee pad on an assisted dip machine take part of your weight as you build strength.

> ❝ BAR DIPS HELP TO BUILD **UPPER-BODY STRENGTH** AND ARE IDEAL IN TRAINING FOR **THROWING EVENTS**. ❞

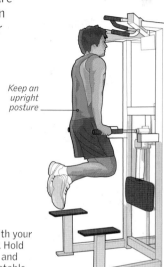

Keep an upright posture

1 Grip the parallel bars with your palms facing each other. Hold your weight on locked arms and cross your feet to keep you stable.

Keep your shoulders over your hands

Keep your hips beneath your shoulders

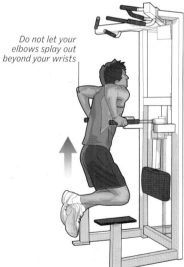

Do not let your elbows splay out beyond your wrists

2 Take a deep breath. Keeping your body straight, unlock your elbows and start to lower your body between the bars, trying to maintain an upright posture.

3 Once you have lowered yourself until your upper arms are parallel to the floor or you cannot go any farther, immediately push up to return to the start position, exhaling as you go.

Arms

Pulley curl

The advantage of performing this exercise on a cable pulley machine instead of using a barbell or dumbbell is that the pulley keeps working your biceps muscles throughout the entire range of motion.

> ❝ THE PULLEY **WORKS YOUR BICEPS MUSCLES** THROUGHOUT THE ENTIRE RANGE OF MOTION. ❞

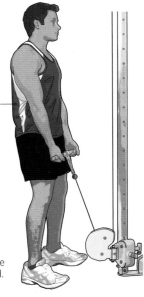

Keep your back straight

1 Set the pulley to a low position. Stand with your knees slightly bent and feet hip-width apart. Grip the bar with your palms forward.

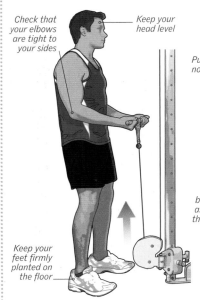

Check that your elbows are tight to your sides

Keep your head level

Keep your feet firmly planted on the floor

2 Raise the bar up toward your chest by bending your arms at your elbows. Breathe out, and do not lean back.

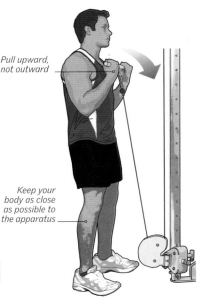

Pull upward, not outward

Keep your body as close as possible to the apparatus

3 Pause briefly at the top of the movement. Lower the bar to rest across your thighs as in the start position.

Arms

Reverse pulley curl

Using a short bar attached to a low pulley makes the reverse curl slightly easier to perform than with free weights. The constant tension provided by the cable challenges the muscles of your forearm in a different way.

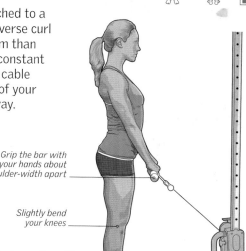

Grip the bar with your hands about shoulder-width apart

Slightly bend your knees

1 Face the low pulley with your feet hip-width apart. Take an overhand grip on the bar, knuckles facing forward.

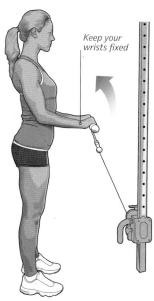

Keep your wrists fixed

2 Raise the bar toward the upper part of your chest, keeping your elbows tight against your body.

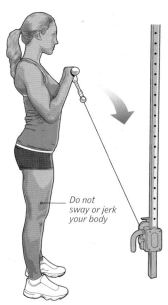

Do not sway or jerk your body

3 Let the bar touch your chest; hold, and lower it back under control to the start position.

Triceps push-down

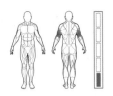

This is a basic exercise for your triceps, the three heads of which form the bulk of your upper arm. Reversing the grip makes this into a pull-down that also works the muscles of your forearms.

Keep your elbows tight to the sides of your body

Bend your knees slightly

1 Set the pulley to a high position, select your desired weight, and take an overhand grip on the bar.

Apply equal pressure to both sides of the bar

Keep your feet flat and slightly apart

2 Push the bar down slowly, using your elbow joints as pivots. Keep your trunk, legs, and hips stationary.

Hold your body upright and do not tilt forward

3 Pause at the bottom of the movement with your triceps fully contracted before returning slowly to the start position.

VARIATION

You can perform the triceps push-down with a rope, a V-bar, or a handle (to work one arm at a time if your arms are not developed evenly). The basic principle is the same in each case. Your elbow joint acts as a pivot and should not move from your side.

Overhead triceps extension

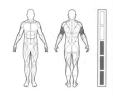

This more advanced exercise works not only your triceps, but also your torso, legs, and shoulders in fixing your body in position. Using the cable allows your triceps to be exercised under tension throughout.

Bend your elbow to an angle of 90 degrees

Hold your upper arms parallel to the floor

1 Select your desired weight on the stack and attach a rope to the high pulley cable. Take up a braced split-leg position. Grip the rope so that your elbows point forward and your arms are tight to the sides of your head.

Keep your spine neutral

Straighten your arms at the end of the movement

Fully contract your triceps

2 From your braced position, with your abs and core muscles tight, extend your arms and contract your triceps in a slow, controlled pull. Keep your torso and hips in the same position throughout.

3 Extend your arms until your triceps are fully contracted, exhaling as you go. Return slowly and under control to the start position, with your hands close to the sides of your head and your body well braced.

Arms

Wrist extension

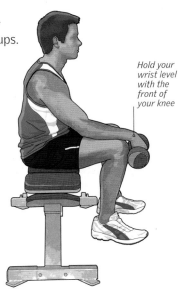

When you work with heavy weights, the weak link in your body may be your grip. This exercise helps to strengthen your forearms, allowing you to hold greater loads for longer periods to work the big muscle groups.

> ❝ THIS EXERCISE **STRENGTHENS YOUR GRIP** AND ALLOWS YOU TO **HOLD GREATER LOADS** FOR LONGER PERIODS. ❞

Hold your wrist level with the front of your knee

1 Sit on a bench holding one dumbbell in an overhand grip. Rest your forearm along the top of your thigh.

Move the dumbbell slowly as high as you can

Maintain a neutral spine

Keep your forearm still

2 Keeping your forearm motionless, use your wrist to raise the dumbbell slowly and under control beyond the horizontal position.

3 Slowly lower the dumbbell to the start position using your wrist alone. Complete the set before repeating with your other arm.

Wrist flexion

Isolating the forearms, this exercise is of great benefit to anyone performing lifting motions, either at the workplace or at a competitive setting.

Keep your torso upright

Let your wrists hang over the front edge of the bench

1 Kneel on the floor or on a mat, facing a bench. Holding a barbell with your palms up, rest your forearms across the bench pad.

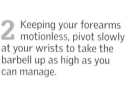

Hold your chest up

Keep your shoulder position fixed

2 Keeping your forearms motionless, pivot slowly at your wrists to take the barbell up as high as you can manage.

3 Lower the barbell slowly to the start position without extending your arms or leaning forward. Keep a strong grip on the bar throughout.

Maintain a tight grip on the barbell

WARNING

Don't let the bar roll toward your fingers in the lowering phase because you run the risk of injuring your wrist or dropping the weight.

Arms

Barbell curl

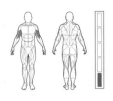

This classic arm exercise develops the strength and size of your biceps muscles. There are numerous variations of the exercise, although the standing barbell curl works your biceps hard throughout the whole range of movement.

Hold the bar in an underhand grip

Keep your body braced and your spine neutral

1 Stand solidly upright, your feet shoulder-width apart, your shoulders down, and your back and chest high.

2 Breathe in and start to curl the bar in an upward arc, keeping your back straight and your elbows tight to the sides of your body. Breathe out on the effort.

3 Curl the bar to the top of your chest. Pause at the top of the movement when your biceps are fully contracted. Your elbows should still be pointing directly down. Return to the start position.

Keep your elbows against your body

WARNING

Be sensible when loading the bar: if the weight is too heavy, you will inevitably start to lean back, using your body momentum rather than your biceps to move the weight. This could damage your spine.

Preacher curl

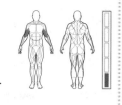

Well defined upper arms are not only impressive, but their strength is also called for in many sports. This exercise totally isolates the showpiece muscles at the front of the upper arms. Because your upper arms rest on the apparatus, shoulder flexion is removed from the lift.

> THIS EXERCISE **ISOLATES THE SHOWPIECE MUSCLES** AT THE FRONT OF THE UPPER ARMS.

Position your armpit on the top of the pad

1 Sit or kneel on the bench with the back of your upper arm on the pad. Grip the dumbbell with your palm facing upward.

Keep your back flat

Keep the back of your upper arm in contact with the pad

2 Raise the dumbbell slowly toward your shoulder through the full range of movement, while inhaling deeply.

3 Lower the dumbbell slowly and under control to the start position. Repeat to complete the set, then change to the other arm.

Hammer dumbbell curl

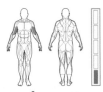

This variation of the barbell curl (see p.86) works your forearms, and is easier on your wrists, which remain in a more natural position. Try it seated on an incline bench to extend the range of movement.

Begin with your arms hanging straight down

Hold your chest high

Keep the dumbbell close to your body

1 Stand with the dumbbells at your sides, hanging on straight arms with your thumbs pointing forward. Pull your shoulders back, keep your chest high and your spine neutral.

2 Curl the dumbbell in an upward arc toward your shoulder. Keep your abs tense and your chest high throughout the whole movement.

Point your elbow straight down

3 Pause for a second at the top of the movement before returning the weight to the start position under control. Work your arms alternately.

WARNING

Ensure that you do not lean back—you will risk damaging your lower back as well as making the exercise less effective. Don't allow your elbows to travel forward because your deltoids will take most of the strain and you won't be working your biceps hard enough.

Incline dumbbell curl

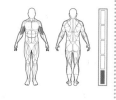

You perform this version of the barbell curl (see p.86) seated on an incline bench, which allows a greater range of movement and more muscle isolation than the basic exercise and injects welcome variety into your arm workout.

Keep your body pressed against the bench and your feet flat on the floor

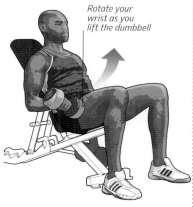

Rotate your wrist as you lift the dumbbell

1 Sit on a bench inclined at a 45-degree angle. Grip a dumbbell in each hand and allow your arms to hang down from your shoulders. Make sure your back is well supported.

2 Curl the dumbbell in one hand in an upward arc toward your shoulder without allowing it to swing. As you do so, slowly turn your inner wrist toward your upper arm.

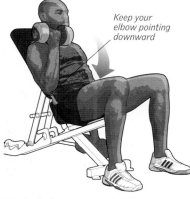

Keep your elbow pointing downward

3 Pause for a second at the top of the movement before returning to the start position with your arm hanging straight down. Repeat with the other arm.

❝ THIS EXERCISE ALLOWS YOU A GREAT RANGE OF MOVEMENT AND INJECTS VARIETY INTO YOUR ARM WORKOUT. ❞

Arms

Dumbbell triceps extension

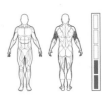

This exercise targets your triceps, which constitute most of the mass of your upper arm. This movement is performed standing and engages your core muscles, providing the added benefit of building trunk strength.

Hold the dumbbell directly above your shoulder

Engage your core muscles

Point your elbow upward

1 Stand with your feet hip-width apart and your knees relaxed. Hold a dumbbell in one hand and raise it overhead to arm's length. Use your free arm to brace across your body.

2 Lower the dumbbell behind your head, keeping your back straight. Pause briefly at the bottom of the motion, then slowly raise the dumbbell to the start position.

VARIATION

If you are a beginner, keeping your body balanced while performing the exercise standing up can be tricky. To improve your stability, try holding on to a solid support with your free hand or carry out the exercise sitting on a bench, preferably one with a back support.

Barbell triceps extension

This exercise works the triceps of both arms simultaneously. You can perform it using a regular barbell or an EZ bar, which lets your wrists and forearms assume a more natural position.

WARNING

Lowering the barbell too fast can cause it to "bounce" off the back of your neck, potentially causing serious damage to your vertebrae. Always work within your capabilities and lower the weight under strict control to the upper-back position.

Engage your core muscles for stability

1 Sit at the end of a bench and hold the barbell overhead with a shoulder-width grip, your knuckles facing backward.

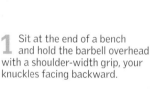

Keep your upper arms stationary

Keep your upper arms close to the sides of your head

2 Slowly and gently lower the barbell behind your head to your upper back until your forearms meet your biceps.

3 Keeping your core muscles tight, straighten your forearms to the start position, moving your arms slowly and under control.

Arms

Close-grip bench press

Although similar to the regular bench press, this exercise places more emphasis on the triceps and anterior deltoids than on the chest due to the closer grip. It helps build big triceps and is a good assistance exercise for competition powerlifting.

1 Lie back on a bench with your head supported and your feet firmly on the floor. Hold an EZ bar with an overhand grip just closer than shoulder width. Extend your arms to hold the bar at upper chest level.

Keep your back flat throughout the exercise

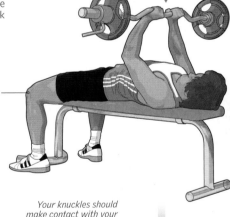

2 Ensuring that the bar is stable and fully under control, unlock your elbows. Then keeping them tucked in, start to lower the bar slowly toward your chest. Breathe in as you do so.

Bend your knees at a right angle

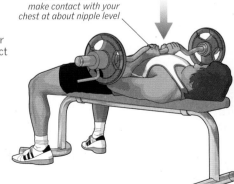

Your knuckles should make contact with your chest at about nipple level

3 Continue lowering the EZ bar until your hands make contact with your chest. Make sure that you grip the bar well. Don't let your elbows flare out, since this will shift the emphasis of the exercise on to your pecs.

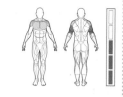

WARNING

You risk serious injury if your muscles fail during the lift. Carry out the close-grip bench press in the presence of a competent and trusted spotter—never alone. Keep your feet in constant contact with the ground; failure to do so may cause you to twist your lower back, causing injury. As ever, be sensible and train within your capabilities.

Keep the bar level and under control

4 Drive the bar to arm's length, keeping it vertically in line with your shoulders. Exhale as you push the bar upward, keeping your elbows tucked in. Push down with your feet.

Push down hard with your feet

Keep the bar vertically over your shoulders

5 Fully extend your arms to the start position; they should lock out at the top of the lift.

Keep your feet firmly on the ground

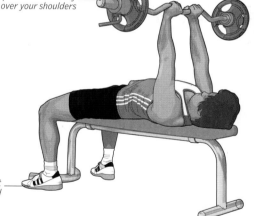

VARIATION

The close grip press-up targets the triceps with a resistance of about two-thirds of your body weight. By adjusting the position of your hands and the direction of your elbows, you can isolate very specific areas of your triceps and deltoids. The exercise is also very safe and does not require the use of any equipment.

Arms

Prone triceps extension

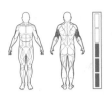

Also known as the "skull crusher" because you bring the bar close to your head, this is a very effective, yet rarely seen, triceps-building exercise. It demands strict technique.

Position your hands so that your knuckles point backward

1 Lie on a bench with your feet flat on the floor and take a shoulder-width grip on the EZ bar with your arms straight above your chest.

Pivot only at the elbow

Keep your core muscles engaged

2 Fix your shoulders and core. Bend only at your elbows—not your shoulders—to lower the barbell slowly just above your forehead.

Do not allow your elbows to splay out

3 Pause at the bottom of the movement. Slowly straighten your forearms under control back to the start position.

Arms

Triceps kickback

With a secure body position, this exercise isolates the triceps. Good technique and a flat back are vital; use a mirror to check that your form is correct.

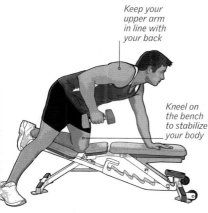

Keep your upper arm in line with your back

Kneel on the bench to stabilize your body

WARNING

While performing this exercise, raise and lower the dumbbell slowly. Swinging the weight can cause twisting of your trunk. This can be very risky, since it can make your lower back unstable and prone to injury.

1 Support your left knee and left hand on a bench; bend from the hips while gripping a dumbbell in your right hand.

Keep your upper body almost parallel to the floor

Hold the weight with an overhand grip

2 Brace your body. Pivot at your elbow to straighten your arm, lifting the weight slowly and under close control to a horizontal position.

3 Pause briefly at the top of the motion; slowly bring the dumbbell back to the start position. Complete the set, then repeat with your other arm.

Front dumbbell raise

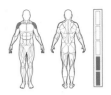

This exercise develops and defines the smaller muscles of your shoulders, which help perform other exercises correctly. You can lift both arms at once or alternate left and right.

Slightly bend your elbows

Rest the dumbbells on the front of your thighs

Keep your head steady and look straight ahead

Brace your abs

Raise the weight to your front, not to your side

1 Stand upright, with your feet hip-width apart and knees soft. Hold the weights in an overhand grip.

2 Keeping your elbows slightly bent and your back straight, raise one dumbbell slowly to the front up to eye level while breathing in.

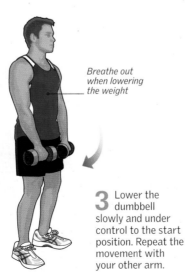

Breathe out when lowering the weight

3 Lower the dumbbell slowly and under control to the start position. Repeat the movement with your other arm.

WARNING

Try not to lean back and swing the dumbbell upward; this not only reduces the effectiveness of the exercise, but could also lead to you injuring your lower back. Instead, switch to a lower weight or try performing the movement with your back against a wall to improve technique.

Shoulders

Lateral dumbbell raise

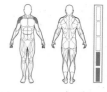

This is a good exercise to develop the width of your upper back and is a valuable aid in most racket and field sports where power—the combination of strength and speed—can give you a competitive edge.

Keep your back straight throughout

Brace your abs

Move the dumbbells up slowly and under control

1 Adopt a hip-width stance, with your knees slightly bent. Hold each dumbbell in front of you, knuckles facing to the side.

2 Engage your core muscles. With your elbows slightly bent, raise both dumbbells to either side of your body up to eye level.

Lift the dumbbells no higher than eye level

Maintain a slight bend in your elbows throughout

3 Pause for a second, then lower the dumbbells slowly and under control back to the start position while breathing out.

" THIS EXERCISE DEVELOPS THE **WIDTH** OF YOUR **UPPER BACK**. IT IS IMPORTANT FOR **RACKET** AND **FIELD SPORTS**. **"**

Shoulders

Military barbell press

The military or barbell press is a simple but very effective exercise. It is one of the basic exercises around which all shoulder routines are constructed.

Engage your core muscles

Keep the bar over your center of gravity

Keep your feet flat on the floor, slightly more than shoulder-width apart

1 Hold the bar across the front of your shoulders. Press the bar upward using your shoulders, moving it in a shallow arc around your face to a position above and slightly behind your head.

2 Gripping tightly, lower the bar back to the start position in the same shallow arc past your head.

WARNING

Ensure that your back is in a neutral position. Bending your back engages your chest, aiding the shoulders, and thus reducing the effectiveness of the exercise. It also places great stress on your lower spine. Keep your wrists rigid and directly under the bar at all times—turning them back can lead to a risk of wrist injury. Finally, take care to move your head back slightly as you lift the bar in order to keep from hitting your chin.

VARIATION

You can perform the military press seated on a bench. The seated position means that you are not able to "help" the bar up by using your legs. Keep your back in an upright position and plant your feet securely on the floor.

Dumbbell shoulder press

You can perform this variant of the shoulder press seated (as shown), standing, or with alternate presses. The main advantage that it offers over the military press is that you do not need to move the bar around your face on the way up and down.

Allow the dumbbells to touch lightly behind your head

Twist the weights on the way up

Engage your core muscles to stabilize your body

Keep your feet flat on the floor

1 Sit on the edge of a bench holding the dumbbells at shoulder height. Press the weights upward to arm's length with your shoulders, breathing out.

2 Briefly hold the weights at arm's length without locking out your elbows. Slowly lower the dumbbells to the start position.

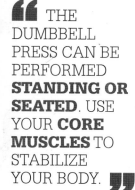

❝ THE DUMBBELL PRESS CAN BE PERFORMED **STANDING OR SEATED**. USE YOUR **CORE MUSCLES** TO STABILIZE YOUR BODY. ❞

VARIATION

If you lack the confidence to use free weights, try the overhead press on a machine. This is a less effective exercise than the seated or standing press, especially if you are training for sports, since your back is supported by the equipment and so you do not engage your stabilizers. Adjust the machine to your height and limb length.

Shoulders

Upright row

This exercise is great for developing strength around your shoulder and upper back, and helps improve your posture. It should be avoided, however, if you suffer from shoulder pain or stiffness.

1 Place your feet hip-width apart and take a narrow overhand grip on the bar, with your palms facing toward your body. Lift the bar so that it rests across your thighs.

2 Pull the bar up toward your chin in a smooth motion. Lift it close to your body, keeping your elbows high and over the bar. Keep your back tight and upright.

3 Continue pulling the bar up until it reaches your chin, keeping your hands below the level of your elbows. Pause briefly at the top of the movement.

Keep your core muscles tight throughout

Do not round your shoulders

Take a narrow grip on the bar to target the trapezius

Plant your feet firmly on the floor

Keep your torso upright

WARNING

The upright row demands good technique if you are to avoid back and shoulder injury, and it should be avoided if you have a history of shoulder pain. Work within your limits and never arch your back or jerk the weight; if you are at all nervous about injury, do not lift the bar above midchest height—this prevents the extreme internal rotation of the shoulder at the top of the movement. Stop this exercise right away if you experience any pain.

Ensure the bar is level throughout

Keep your knees slightly bent

4 Lower the bar to the start position under close control. Use a smooth motion, keeping your elbows over the bar and your back tight.

Keep your body upright

5 Return to the start position with your arms fully extended. Exhale slowly as you do so. Return the bar to the floor at the end of your set.

VARIATION

Using dumbbells for the upright row works each arm independently, and prevents your elbows from rising much farther than parallel to the floor, making this an easier exercise if you are less flexible in the shoulders.

VARIATION

Using a low cable pulley offers you a steadier resistance through the movement than if you were to use a barbell. Make sure that you stand close to the pulley and keep the bar tight to your body. Use a close grip to work your upper back, or a wider grip to engage your shoulders in the exercise.

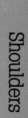

Shoulders

Rear lateral raise

This is a great raw strength exercise that develops your shoulders and the muscles in the middle section of your back—principally your rhomboids. You can perform the exercise standing, seated, or lying, but in all cases ensure that you maintain good body position to keep from engaging the larger muscles of your back.

Keep your spine in a neutral position

Brace your abs and back muscles

Keep your shoulders down and your neck extended

Slightly bend your elbows

Place your feet hip-width apart

1 Slightly bend your knees. Keeping your back flat, drop your torso forward with your head looking to the front and a little down. Flex your elbows slightly and rest the plates of the dumbbells on your upper thighs.

2 Lift the dumbbells away from your body in a smooth motion with the weights moving symmetrically. Keep the weights in line with your shoulders and ensure that your back stays tight. Breathe out on exertion.

❝ IT DEVELOPS THE MUSCLES IN THE MIDDLE SECTION OF YOUR BACK. ❞

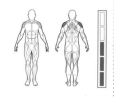

Rounding your back during this exercise may cause injury to your back or spine. Keep the movement of the weights slow and well balanced on both sides, trying not to move your knees, head, or spine; your elbows should be slightly bent and fixed at this angle throughout. Do not allow your shoulders to rise.

Raise the weights to the level of your shoulders or just above

Try not to move your torso during the lift

Keep your spine neutral

Keep your core muscles tight

Grip the dumbbells with your palms facing in

3 Bring the dumbbells up level with your shoulders while depressing your shoulder blades. Hold your position briefly at the top of the motion. Continue to breathe freely.

4 Reverse the motion under tight control, returning the dumbbells to the start position. Resist the weights on the way down rather than letting them drop under gravity. Breathe in during the return phase.

VARIATION

Performing this exercise lying prone on a bench puts more emphasis on your medial deltoids and rhomboids. This variant is best performed with your legs fixed, isolating the target muscles further. You may also perform the exercise sitting at the end of a bench; here, keep your torso bent over to work your posterior deltoids, or more upright to emphasize your medial deltoids.

Shoulders

Squat

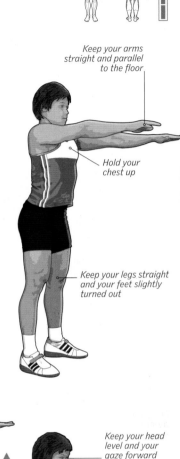

This is the key mobilizer for your lower body and core, and is also an essential warm-up for the squatting movement around which so much of strength training and power work is based. Maintaining good technique is essential: go as low as possible to improve your range of motion and do not "bounce" at the bottom of the squat.

> ❝ A **KEY MOBILIZER** FOR **LOWER BODY AND CORE**, THIS EXERCISE IS A CRUCIAL **WARM-UP** FOR THE SQUATTING MOVEMENT. ❞

Keep your arms straight and parallel to the floor

Hold your chest up

Keep your legs straight and your feet slightly turned out

1 Start from a position in which your body is upright, your spine is neutral, and your feet are slightly wider than shoulder-width.

Ease your hips back

Face your palms downward

The bend in your knees should be in line with your feet

Keep your head level and your gaze forward

Hold your torso upright throughout the exercise

2 Breathe in and bend at your knees and hips, allowing your hips to ease backward. Keep your spine neutral and your gaze level.

3 Squat down until your thighs are parallel to the floor (or farther if you have the mobility). Return to the start position.

Forward lunge

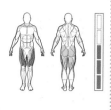

This full-body exercise is effective in developing strength in your leg and hip muscles. Holding the dumbbells by your sides rather than over your shoulders makes it easier for you to hold your body upright. Be sure to practice the movement before using weights.

Engage your stabilizer muscles to keep your core tight

Position your feet hip-width apart

Pull your shoulders back

Keep your back leg straight

1 Keep your body upright, your spine neutral, your chest high, and your shoulders back. Hold a dumbbell in each hand, with your arms by your sides.

2 Take a step forward, holding your upper body upright. Descend under tight control by bending at your hips, knees, and ankles. Don't lean forward at any point.

3 Descend until both knees reach an angle of 90 degrees. Your back knee should be directly under your hip and just off the floor. Hold before you return to the start position.

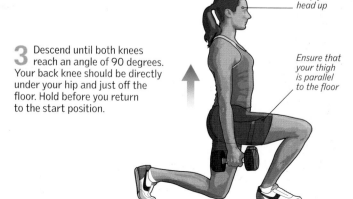

Keep your head up

Ensure that your thigh is parallel to the floor

45-degree leg press

This movement is good for beginners who are preparing for more functional leg exercises, such as the squat. It places little stress on the lower back and is suitable for those who have not yet developed high core strength. It allows heavy weights to be used early on, providing motivation to the novice. As when using all exercise machines, ensure that the leg press is set to match your height and limb length.

1 Select your desired weight and sit on the machine. Place your feet hip-width apart on the platform and take the weight on your legs. Release the safety lock on the machine, and hold the handle supports.

Bend your knees to a 90-degree angle

Keep your head and back well supported on the pad

2 Extend your legs to push the platform away from you. Push slowly, keeping your heels and toes on the platform; do not allow your knees to splay outward as you push.

Position your feet evenly on the platform

Align your knees with your feet

3 Continue pushing until your legs are almost fully extended. Pause for a moment at the top of the movement and then return to the start position slowly and under control.

Keep your heels and toes pressed against the platform

Extend your legs almost fully

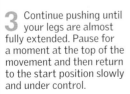

Calf raise

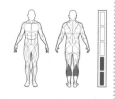

This exercise develops the muscles of your lower leg. The movement tests your balance, especially when carried out with heavier free weights, so work on a Smith machine to stabilize your body.

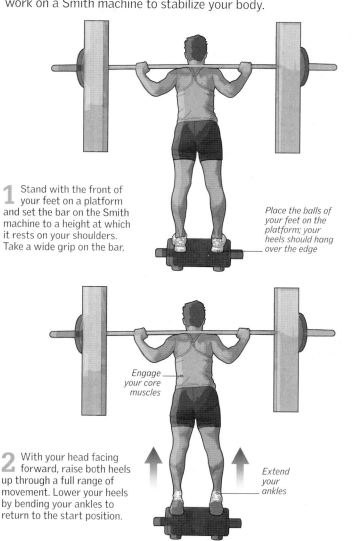

1 Stand with the front of your feet on a platform and set the bar on the Smith machine to a height at which it rests on your shoulders. Take a wide grip on the bar.

Place the balls of your feet on the platform; your heels should hang over the edge

Engage your core muscles

2 With your head facing forward, raise both heels up through a full range of movement. Lower your heels by bending your ankles to return to the start position.

Extend your ankles

VARIATION

This exercise can be performed on a calf raise machine on which you lift weighted pads. Set the resistance and stand under the pads, gripping the handles and keeping your elbows bent. Contract your calf muscles and extend your ankles. Hold the top position before lowering your body under full control.

Legs

Machine leg extension

This exercise isolates the quads—the largest muscle group in your body—as you flex and extend your legs at the knee joints. Quads work to straighten the knees, so this exercise can help protect your knees or assist with rehabilitation after a knee injury.

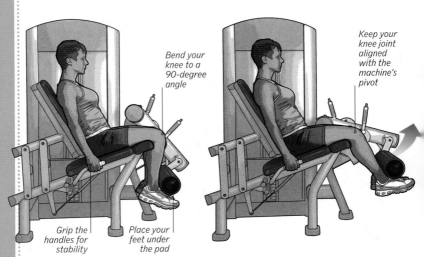

Bend your knee to a 90-degree angle

Keep your knee joint aligned with the machine's pivot

Grip the handles for stability

Place your feet under the pad

1 Select a weight from the stack and sit on the machine with your back against the pad. Adjust the moving pad to suit the length of your lower leg.

2 Using a controlled movement—and no jerking—bring your lower leg up while pressing your back and buttocks against the pads.

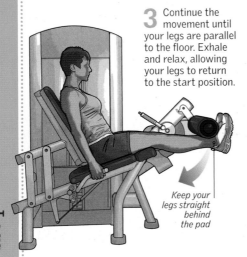

3 Continue the movement until your legs are parallel to the floor. Exhale and relax, allowing your legs to return to the start position.

Keep your legs straight behind the pad

❝ THE MACHINE LEG EXTENSION **ISOLATES THE QUADS** AS YOU **FLEX AND EXTEND YOUR LEGS** AT THE KNEE JOINTS. THIS EXERCISE CAN HELP PROTECT YOUR KNEES. ❞

Machine leg curl

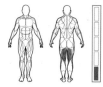

The leg curl, usually carried out on a machine, either sitting or lying face down, is a good exercise for the hamstrings; working these muscles balances the development of the quads on the front of your legs.

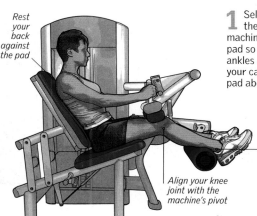

Rest your back against the pad

Align your knee joint with the machine's pivot

Place your ankles on the pad of the moving arm

1 Select a weight from the stack and sit on the machine. Adjust the moving pad so that it is under your ankles and doesn't slide up your calves. Position the lap pad above your knees.

Keep the pad behind your ankles

2 Bring the moving arm back in a smooth motion to contract your hamstrings fully, then return it under control to the start position. Keep your back stable against the seat.

VARIATION

You can carry out a similar exercise using a cable pulley machine. This is more challenging because you have to stabilize your whole body—the machine does not support you in a fixed position. Attach an ankle strap and ensure that the knee of your moving leg points down so that your hamstring pulls your heel toward your glutes.

Move slowly, taking slightly longer to lower your leg than to raise it.

Legs

Back squat

This multi-joint exercise is extremely effective at developing the muscles of your legs. It is a great foundation exercise for building overall power and strength, but must be performed with good technique.

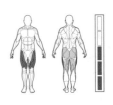

Maintain a neutral spine

Place your feet just wider than shoulder-width apart

Hold your chest high

Gaze straight ahead

1 Take a balanced grip on the bar in the rack. Duck beneath it and stand with your feet directly under the bar. Step back and stand up straight with the bar resting on the upper part of your back.

2 Breathe deeply, and tensing your abs and glutes, start the descent. Keep your feet pointing outward and let your knees follow the angle of your feet as you bend them and ease your hips back.

Tense up the stabilizers in your back and abs

Keep the bar centered over your feet

Maintain a neutral back position

Keep the bar stable and level

3 Keep bending at your knees with your spine in a neutral position. Lower your body slowly and under tight control as you ease your hips farther back. Keep your knees over your toes.

4 Continue bending at your knees, easing your hips back until your thighs are parallel to the floor. Your body should now be at a 45-degree angle. Return to the start position, breathing out.

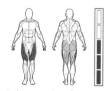

Front barbell squat

In this key multi-joint exercise, you position the weight on the front of your shoulders. It demands a more upright body posture than the back squat and places more emphasis on your quads and core.

Brace your hips and engage your core muscles

Hold the bar across your collar bone and deltoids

Point your elbows forward

Bend your knees in line with your out-turned feet

1 Take the bar from a rack with your hands outside your shoulders, or clean it (see pp.122–23) to your shoulders. Stand upright and keep your feet a little more than shoulder-width apart and slightly out-turned.

2 With your chest held high, take a deep breath and start to bend at the knees, easing your hips back and keeping your elbows pointing forward.

Keep a relatively upright body position

Gaze straight ahead

Ease your hips back as you flex at your knees

3 Keep your head level, your back flat, and your chest high, squatting down until your thighs are parallel to the floor, or as close as possible. Return to the start position, breathing out as you stand.

WARNING

Keep your body at the same upright angle throughout the movement and do not allow your heels to lift off the floor. Ensure that you do not drop your elbows or let them touch your knees at the bottom of the lift. Never sacrifice good technique by overloading the bar with weight.

Legs

Barbell deadlift

Sometimes called the "king of exercises" because of its effectiveness in building leg and back strength, the deadlift is also one of the three lifts performed in competitive powerlifting.

Grip the bar with an alternate hook—one hand over, and the other under the bar

Keep your back flat and tight throughout

1 Squat down so that your feet are under the bar, and the bar rests against your shins. Grip the bar using an alternate hook grip to prevent it from rotating; your hands should be wider than shoulder-width apart.

Pull your shoulder blades together

Keep the bar close to your body throughout the lift

Push your hips in toward the bar

2 Begin lifting the bar with a long, strong leg push, extending your knees and hips. Your knees should be bent as you lift the bar past them.

Drive off your feet

Ensure that your feet remain firmly planted flat on the floor

WARNING

Correct lifting technique is essential in this movement. Never lift with your spine flexed forward: not only will the exercise be ineffective, but you will also risk spinal injury. Always raise and lower your shoulders and hips together. Keep the bar close to your body and do not drop it at the end of the movement; always lower it under control.

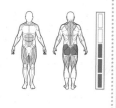

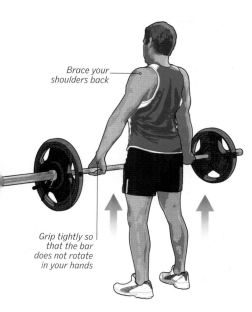

Brace your shoulders back

Grip tightly so that the bar does not rotate in your hands

3 Continue the lift as if pushing the floor away from yourself with your feet, until you stand up straight with your knees locked.

Lower the bar under control

Move your hips back and down

4 Unlock your knees. Maintaining a tight, flat back and keeping your head up, start to lower the bar under control. Your knees should be bent as you lower the bar past them.

Pull your shoulders back

Bend at your knees

5 Slowly move your hips and shoulders together when lowering the bar back down to the start position. Do not drop the bar.

Overhead barbell lunge

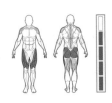

This exercise tests your balance and brings the muscles of your shoulders and back into play. It is an excellent exercise for developing strength and power for contact sports.

1 Stand upright with your feet hip-width apart. Hold the barbell overhead with a wide grip, knuckles facing backward, and your elbows slightly bent.

Hold the weight in line with your shoulder joints

Stabilize your torso by tightening your core muscles

Keep your front foot flat

Bend your knee so that it is directly over your foot

2 Engage your core muscles and take a long step forward, lowering your rear knee so that it almost touches the floor. Breathe freely at all times.

3 Pause, then straighten your front leg and step back, maintaining the stance at hip width. Return to the start position; finish your set before switching legs.

Straight-leg deadlift

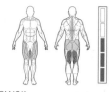

This underestimated exercise strengthens your lower back and develops your legs and glutes. Many football linebackers include this in their workout regimen.

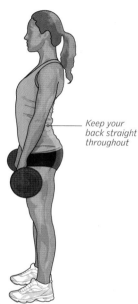

Keep your back straight throughout

Engage your core muscles

1 Stand upright with your feet hip-width apart and the barbell resting across your upper thighs. Hold the bar with an overhand grip.

2 Keep your head facing forward and your knees almost locked. Then bend gently from your waist to lower the barbell. Inhale as you do this movement.

3 Maintaining control over your core stability, slowly pivot at your hips to raise your upper body to the start position. Breathe out as you do so.

VARIATION

If you have good hip mobility, try standing on an elevated platform. This will allow the barbell to travel beyond the level of your feet and make your muscles work harder. However, do not be tempted to extend your muscles beyond what feels comfortable. Always try to keep your motion fluid, without "bouncing" the barbell.

Legs

Dumbbell split squat

This exercise builds on the basic lunge movement (see pp.48–49) but allows you to lift more weight. It is valuable for developing hip mobility and good shoulder posture as well as strength in your quads.

> " THIS EXERCISE BUILDS ON THE **BASIC LUNGE MOVEMENT** AND DEVELOPS **HIP MOBILITY** AND **GOOD SHOULDER POSTURE**. "

1 Maintain a standing position with your feet shoulder-width apart and your arms hanging by your sides. Then take a stride forward, keeping your chest high and looking straight ahead.

Hold the dumbbells between your feet

Rise up on your toes on the rear foot and keep your front foot flat

Keep your body upright throughout the movement

Use your lead leg to carry most of your weight

Shrug your shoulders back and keep your spine neutral

Hold your chest high

Keep your rear foot on tiptoe

2 Flex at your knee and hip, and drop slowly into a split position. Your front knee should not move beyond your toes and your rear knee should not touch the ground.

3 Return to the start position and perform the required number of reps on one leg before switching to the other and repeating the sequence.

Overhead split squat

Holding a barbell overhead demands good shoulder and hip mobility but the payoff is that your body functions as a unit and you strengthen your core as well as your legs.

Push upward against the bar with your elbows locked

1 Begin in a standing position with your feet shoulder-width apart. Press the weight overhead and take a stride forward.

Keep the weight over the center of gravity between your feet

2 Drop slowly into the split position, ensuring that your front knee does not go beyond your toes and your rear knee doesn't touch the floor.

Hold the weight directly over your shoulder joints

3 Straighten your front leg to return to the start position. After you have completed your set, switch legs and repeat on the other side.

Barbell step-up

This excellent exercise targets the main muscles of your leg—the quads, hamstrings, and glutes. The muscles of your calves assist while your core muscles stop your body from leaning forward or twisting. The exercise helps develop, and also puts demands on, your heart and lungs. Beginners should start with body weight until they are familiar with the movement.

❝ THIS EXERCISE TARGETS YOUR QUADS, HAMSTRINGS, AND GLUTES. IT ALSO HELPS YOUR HEART AND LUNGS. ❞

Look straight ahead

Take a deep breath before starting the exercise

Hold your body upright

Maintain a relaxed leg position

Keep your feet shoulder-width apart

Keep the bar stable across your shoulders

Hold your chest up throughout

Bend your knee to a 90-degree angle

Keep your heel flat on the floor

1 Facing a bench, load a barbell on to the top of your shoulders behind your neck. Grasp the bar with your hands just wider than shoulder-width apart, and take a solid upright stance with your feet parallel.

2 Step up on to the bench with your left foot ensuring that your heel is not hanging over the edge. The bench should be high enough to allow an angle of 90 degrees at your knee joint.

VARIATION

Try this exercise holding dumbbells at your sides. They are easier to "load" and hold in place than a barbell and can be safely jettisoned if you start to feel yourself losing balance. You can also make this exercise easier by using just your own body weight to work against gravity.

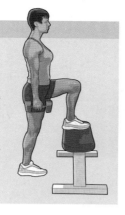

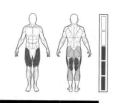

WARNING

Keep you back straight and avoid leaning forward or twisting your body when you are stepping up and down. Do not "round" your back.

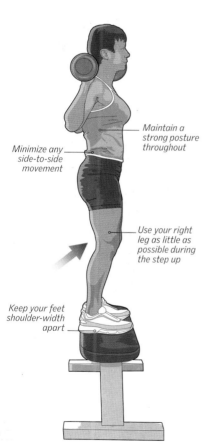

Minimize any side-to-side movement

Maintain a strong posture throughout

Use your right leg as little as possible during the step up

Keep your feet shoulder-width apart

Keep the bar secure on your shoulders

Maintain your balance

Lean forward a little

Point your toe toward the floor

3 Push down with your left heel and use your left thigh and glute muscles to lift your right foot up on to the bench. Drive your body up, exhaling as you do so.

4 Step down off the bench with your right leg first. Ensure that you keep your body upright and your chest high. Finish the set leading with one leg, then switch to the other.

Bulgarian barbell split squat

This advanced exercise was designed by the Bulgarian National Weightlifting squad to develop strength, balance, and flexibility.

Engage your core muscles

Rest your foot on top of the bench

1 Begin with the barbell resting on your upper back and your legs hip-width apart. Bend one leg and rest it on a bench behind you.

Breathe freely on descent

2 Slowly lower your rear knee toward the floor. Stop the movement when the top of your front thigh is parallel to the floor.

Keep your torso upright during the squat

Your rear knee almost meets the floor at the bottom of the motion

3 From the bottom of the movement, straighten your front leg to the standing position; do not "lock" your knee. Complete your set and repeat on your other leg.

Legs

Good morning barbell

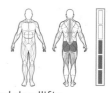

You can use this exercise to prepare for squats and deadlifts. It works the glutes and hamstrings, while the large spinal erector muscles hold your back flat. As your flexibility increases, you may be able to lower your upper body so that it is parallel to the floor.

Plant your heels on the floor

Support the bar with your upper arms

1 Holding your body upright, position the barbell behind your neck and on your upper back. Keep your knees slightly bent and your spine neutral.

2 Bending slightly at your knees and hips, start to lean forward under control. Keep your chin up—it will stop you from rounding your back.

Keep your spine neutral

3 Lean forward by pivoting at your hip. Continue lowering your chest, keeping your back neutral and allowing your knees to bend slightly.

4 Flex as far as possible: with practice your back may be parallel to the floor. Return to the start position, breathing out as you go.

Legs

Power clean

Though technically difficult, this explosive exercise is a fantastic all-around power-builder; when performed with lighter weights. It also makes an excellent warm-up.

1 Squat with your feet hip-width apart under the bar, and your hips higher than your knees. Grip the barbell overhand, palms just wider than shoulder-width apart.

2 Raise the bar above your knees; push in your hips while driving up hard with your legs to give the weight momentum.

Keep your shoulders over the bar for as long as possible

Let the bar touch the top of your thighs

3 Forcefully extend your hips, knees, and ankles, keeping the bar close to your body. Shrug your shoulders upward hard.

Drop your elbows when your shoulders reach their highest point

Keep the bar close to your body

Your toes may leave the floor as you drive up explosively

4 On reaching full extension, lower your body under the bar, and drop and rotate your elbows down.

Rotate your arms around the bar

Punch your elbows forward to fix the bar

Tense your core muscles to stabilize your body

Drop into a semi-squat

5 Flex your hips and knees into a semi-squat and catch the bar on the top of your shoulders. Stand up straight by extending your legs.

Control the descent of the bar

6 Keeping your back flat, let the weight down under control to your thighs, and return the bar to the floor.

WARNING

Perform all the dynamic lifts on a proper lifting platform. This complex movement demands excellent technique, balance, and control. Practice with light weights until perfect, and, if possible, spend time with a qualified weight-lifting coach.

Keep your feet flat on the floor

Legs

Power snatch

This fast, technically tough exercise is ideal for improving all-around power. Make sure to practice the movement with light weights initially.

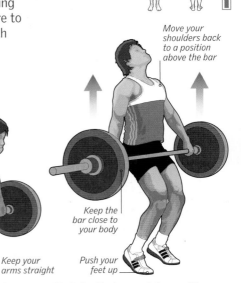

Move your shoulders back to a position above the bar

Keep your hips higher than your knees

Keep your arms straight

1 Squat with your feet hip-width apart under the bar. Grip the bar overhand with your hands as close to the weight collars as possible.

Keep the bar close to your body

Push your feet up

2 Raise the bar; push in your hips while driving up hard with your legs to give the weight momentum.

Keep the bar close to your body

Strongly pull yourself up; your feet may leave the floor as you do so

3 Forcefully extend your hips, knees, and ankles, while keeping the bar close to your body. Shrug your shoulders upward hard.

Slightly bend your arms to let the bar past your head

4 Lower your body underneath, as you lift the bar up, while rotating your elbows downward and under the bar.

Push the barbell to its highest point by straightening your legs

Lock out your arms

Engage your core muscles to stabilize your body

Bend at your knees in a shallow squat

Keep your feet flat on the floor, hip-width apart

5 Squat just low enough to catch the bar at arm's length. Punch your arms straight and catch the bar on "hard locked" elbows.

6 Keep the bar stable and balanced on your locked arms before standing up with the weight overhead. Keep your back tight and your head up.

Keep your back flat and firm

Bend your knees as you lower the bar to your thighs

7 Lower the bar, keeping it close to your body. Bend your knees and catch the bar on your upper thighs before lowering it to the floor.

WARNING

The power snatch is an explosive lift, even faster than the power clean. You can injure your back if your technique is poor. Keep a flat, tight back at all times throughout this exercise.

❝ THE POWER SNATCH IS FASTER THAN THE POWER CLEAN AND IS IDEAL FOR IMPROVING ALL-AROUND POWER. ❞

Abdominal crunch

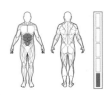

The basic abdominal crunch is one of the simplest and most popular of all exercises. It helps you to develop a strong core and improves your posture, but you must ensure you have good technique.

1 Lie on a mat with your knees bent, your feet flat, and your fingers against the sides of your head.

Keep your chin up and your neck extended

2 Engage your core and raise your upper back and shoulders slightly off the floor. Hold for a moment.

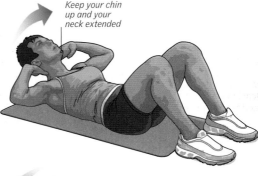

3 Lower your upper body slowly to the floor; don't let your body's momentum or gravity drive your movement.

Keep your hips stable throughout

VARIATION

To work your abdominal area more effectively, use a pulsing action. Pause your crunch at the top of the movement and slide your hands up and down your thighs. The movement involved in each pulse is very small, but squeeze your abs just a little bit tighter each time. Perform around five "pulses" per crunch repetition.

Sit-up

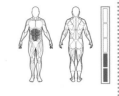

The classic sit-up is still used in many training programs. It is a good abdominal exercise but should be avoided if you have any lower back problems or have a weak core.

Bend your elbows and place your fingers against your temples

1 Lie on your back with both feet flat on the floor and your knees bent to reduce stress on your spine.

Avoid swinging yourself up

2 Engage your core muscles and raise your torso upward, leaving your buttocks and feet on the floor.

Strongly contract your abs and breathe out as you rise

3 Pause at the upright position, then slowly lower your upper body to the floor back to the start position.

Curl in your shoulders

VARIATION

Resting your legs on a bench isolates your abdominals during the sit-up exercise, providing a more intense abdominal workout.

Keep your feet flat on the floor

Core and abs

Reverse crunch

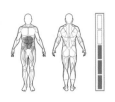

In this version of the abdominal crunch (see p.126), you move your legs rather than your torso. It is good for the lower abs as well as the rectus femoris and the hip flexors, and is appropriate for many sports as a general conditioning exercise.

> ❝ THIS VERSION OF THE ABDOMINAL CRUNCH IS GOOD FOR THE **LOWER ABS**, **RECTUS FEMORIS**, AND THE **HIP FLEXORS**. ❞

Grip the bench for stability

Bend your knees and keep them pressed together

1 Lie with your head, shoulders, and buttocks in contact with the surface of a stable bench. Flex your hips and knees to a right angle.

Pause briefly at the top of the motion

2 Extend your legs and slowly lift your buttocks off the bench. Use your abs to do this, rather than the momentum of your legs.

Keep your feet together

3 Contract your abs hard and lower your legs slowly to the start position; your buttocks should just make contact with the bench.

90-90 crunch

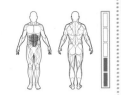

This fairly easy abdominal crunch puts emphasis on the upper part of your rectus abdominus muscles and takes pressure off your lower back. Perform it with your knees bent and feet fixed.

WARNING

Be sure to place your feet on top of the bench. Do not hook them underneath to provide leverage; this will place great stress on your lower back. Do not pull on your head or neck when performing this exercise and ensure that your lower back and buttocks remain in contact with the floor. Do not fling your head or arms forward when your abdominal muscles start to tire.

Start with your head, shoulders, and buttocks in contact with the floor

1 Lie flat, with your hips and knees bent at 90 degrees. Rest your calves on a bench, hooking your heels over the edge.

Rest your fingers lightly on the sides of your head

2 Inhale deeply and lift your shoulders off the floor; actively contract your abdominal muscles, curling your torso toward your knees.

Keep your heels hooked over the edge of the bench

3 Exhale, and hold at the top of the movement for a second. Lower your torso back to the starting position under tight control.

VARIATION

Try this exercise with a twist. Turn your torso slightly to one side as you rise. Aim your left elbow at your right knee. This variation will also work your oblique muscles.

Core and abs

Figure-4 crunch

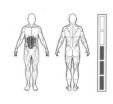

This fairly advanced exercise targets
your rectus abdominis and external oblique
muscles. It is a good general conditioning
exercise useful for multiple sports.

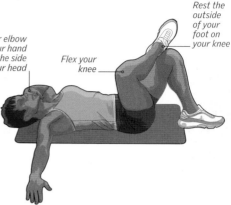

*Bend your elbow
and rest your hand
lightly on the side
of your head*

*Flex your
knee*

*Rest the
outside
of your
foot on
your knee*

1 Lie on an exercise mat
with your knees bent.
Extend your right arm on the
floor for balance, and cross
your right leg over the left.

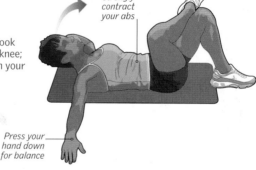

*Strongly
contract
your abs*

2 Lift your head and look
toward your flexed knee;
at the same time tighten your
abs and start bringing
your left elbow up.

*Press your
hand down
for balance*

WARNING

You need good flexibility
to assume the start
position of this exercise.
Do not try to force your
body to do so; modify the
exercise so that you are
comfortable, and perform
suitable mobility exercises
to make you more supple
(see pp.41–43). At no
stage of the exercise
should you pull on your
head or neck—this can
lead to spinal injury.

3 Bring your left elbow
and your flexed knee
toward one another. Pause
and then return under control
to the start position.

V-leg raise

This exercise provides a powerful workout for your abdominal muscles; you can boost the intensity further by placing a weight between your ankles. Ensure that the platform or bench you use is sufficiently stable.

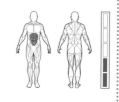

Balance your body on the edge of the bench

Contract your hamstrings, quads, and calf muscles

66 THIS EXERCISE PROVIDES A **POWERFUL WORKOUT** FOR YOUR **ABDOMINAL MUSCLES**. 99

1 Sit on the bench, supporting yourself by gripping the pad behind you. Lift your legs together, keeping your toes pointed.

Maintain your position by contracting the muscles in your shoulder girdle

Bend your knees

Point your toes away from your body

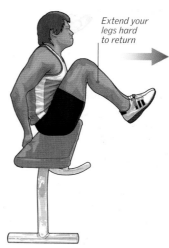

Extend your legs hard to return

2 Keeping your feet and knees together, bend your knees, and bring them toward your chest. Pull your torso forward a little for balance.

3 Bring your knees as close to your body as possible. Return by extending your hips and knees and leaning back to counterbalance.

Core and abs

Prone plank

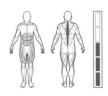

This static floor exercise (also called the bridge) engages your core and many major muscle groups of your upper and lower body in maintaining a static position. This exercise can be used to prevent lower back problems.

Keep your feet together

Rest your forearms against the floor

1 Lie face down on an exercise mat with your elbows to your sides and your palms alongside your head, facing down.

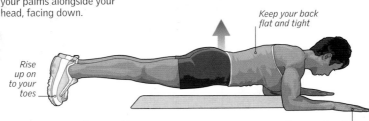

Keep your back flat and tight

Rise up on to your toes

Keep your hands flat on the floor

2 Engaging your core and leg muscles, raise your body from the floor, supporting your weight on your forearms and toes while breathing freely.

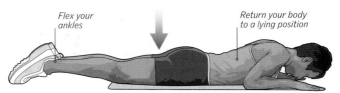

Flex your ankles

Return your body to a lying position

3 Hold the plank position for a short while—try 20 seconds to start with—then gently lower your body back on to the exercise mat.

VARIATION

You can make the exercise more challenging by simultaneously extending one arm and the opposite leg from the plank position. This position, called the "Superman," demands excellent balance. Conversely,

the exercise can be made easier to perform by supporting your lower body on your knees rather than on your toes.

Core and abs

Side plank

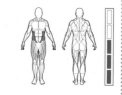

This is an excellent exercise for developing the muscles located to the sides of your torso, vital in maintaining good posture in most activities. This exercise is easy to do at home and helps tone the waist.

1 Lie side on, supporting your weight on your feet and forearm. Ensure that your upper arm is vertical, your forearm is perpendicular to your body, and your legs are straight.

Rest your lower arm along your hips

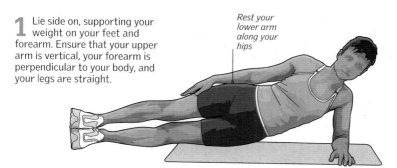

2 Gently raise your hips off the floor to a point where your head and spinal column are in line. At the same time, raise your upper arm to a vertical position while breathing freely.

Balance on the sides of your stacked feet

3 Hold for around 20 seconds, then slowly lower your upper arm to your side and your hips to the floor. Repeat as required before switching sides.

Hold your glutes and core tight

Core and abs

Roman chair side bend

Targeting your obliques, this exercise is best performed on a Roman chair—a piece of apparatus that has a ledge behind which you can secure your feet. It may also be done on a regular bench, in which case you will need a partner to hold your feet.

Hold your hands at head level or crossed over your chest

1 Lie sideways on the Roman chair; adjust it so that your upper body can pivot comfortably at your hips toward the floor.

Move from side-to-side

2 Lean slowly sideways toward the floor, as far as is comfortable. Make sure not to lean forward or back. Breathe in on the descent.

Breathe out on the upward movement

3 Pause at full extension, then gently raise your body to the start position. Complete the set for one side and repeat on the other.

Ball crunch

Performing abdominal crunches on a stability ball helps you keep your abs contracted throughout the entire exercise. You need to work constantly to fix your body in position using your deep core muscles on the inherently unstable ball.

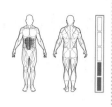

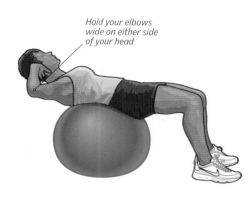

Hold your elbows wide on either side of your head

1 Begin with your feet flat on the floor and your knees bent at a 90-degree angle. Rest your hands on the sides of your head.

Rest your hands lightly on your head

Keep your back straight

2 Push your lower back into the ball, contract your abs and lift your shoulders a few inches, crunching your abs toward your hips.

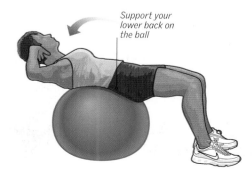

Support your lower back on the ball

3 Lower your torso under tight control, still keeping the tension in your abs. Make sure not to "flop" back on to the ball.

Core and abs

Ball twist

This exercise builds strong abs and strengthens the rotational muscles of your torso. Working on the ball also promotes balance, making this a great exercise for activities such as golf and surfing.

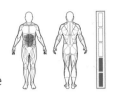

1 Lie on the stability ball with your lower back well supported. Keep your feet flat on the floor and your knees at an angle of about 90 degrees. Hold your hands to the sides of your head.

Do not pull your head forward with your hands

Use your feet to help stabilize your body

2 Once you feel steady and stable, begin to crunch up. About halfway up, twist your torso to one side—spreading your elbows wide helps you to balance.

Place your fingers lightly against the sides of your head

Strongly contract your abs

3 Hold the top position for around one second, then return to the start position. Keeping your lower body still, lower and untwist your upper body.

Ball back extension

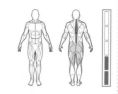

This exercise helps to balance your trunk by conditioning your lower back muscles that work opposite your abs. A strong trunk provides good protection against back injury.

WARNING

Before starting the exercise, check that the ball is the correct size for your limb length. You should be able to touch the floor with straight arms. Keep your movement smooth and controlled; if you straighten your torso too quickly you risk compressing the vertebrae in your back and damaging your sciatic nerve. Do not pull your torso above the natural line of your spine—hyperextending your back may be risky.

1 Lie with your abs and upper thighs "wrapped" across the ball, with the tips of your toes touching the floor.

2 With the tips of your fingers touching the sides of your head, slowly straighten your body while breathing in.

Move your elbows back a little on ascent

Keep your knees slightly bent

Control your descent by contracting the muscles of your back

3 Gently and smoothly lower your upper body to the start position while breathing out.

Keep your toes in contact with the floor

Core and abs

Ball press-up

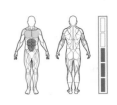

In this exercise, you elevate your feet on to the Swiss ball to make your chest, shoulders, and upper arms work harder than in a regular push-up (see p.52). The core stabilizers of your torso and hips are also fully engaged, keeping your body in alignment, while your feet are supported on the inherently unstable ball.

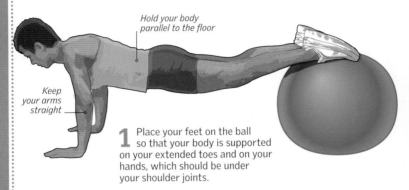

Hold your body parallel to the floor

Keep your arms straight

1 Place your feet on the ball so that your body is supported on your extended toes and on your hands, which should be under your shoulder joints.

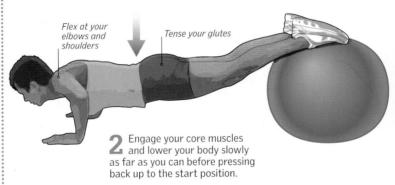

Flex at your elbows and shoulders

Tense your glutes

2 Engage your core muscles and lower your body slowly as far as you can before pressing back up to the start position.

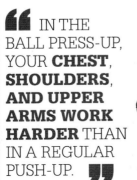

❝ IN THE BALL PRESS-UP, YOUR **CHEST, SHOULDERS, AND UPPER ARMS WORK HARDER** THAN IN A REGULAR PUSH-UP. **❞**

WARNING

Your body should be straight throughout this exercise. Don't allow your midsection to droop toward the floor because you'll place great stress on your back. Exhaling while you push up and inhaling as you lower your torso will help you keep good technique.

Ball jackknife

This valuable but relatively advanced exercise demands great balance and control. It works the core muscles that flex your hips and also stresses your abdominal muscles.

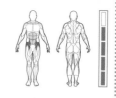

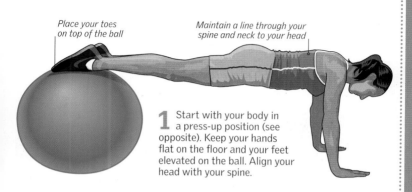

Place your toes on top of the ball

Maintain a line through your spine and neck to your head

1 Start with your body in a press-up position (see opposite). Keep your hands flat on the floor and your feet elevated on the ball. Align your head with your spine.

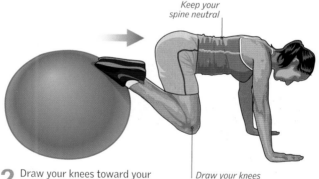

Keep your spine neutral

2 Draw your knees toward your chest, maintaining a neutral spine as the ball rolls forward. Your hips will rise a little as the ball moves.

Draw your knees toward your chest

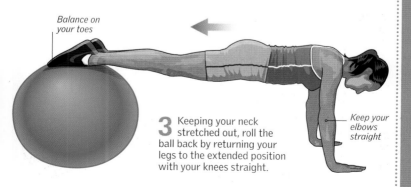

Balance on your toes

3 Keeping your neck stretched out, roll the ball back by returning your legs to the extended position with your knees straight.

Keep your elbows straight

Core and abs

Woodchop

This powerful rotational exercise develops the muscles of your trunk, making it ideal for training in sports that involve a twisting motion, such as throwing or hitting a ball with a bat or racket.

> ❝ THE WOODCHOP IS A **POWERFUL ROTATIONAL EXERCISE** THAT DEVELOPS THE **MUSCLES OF YOUR TRUNK**. ❞

Keep both of your hands above your shoulders

Adopt a comfortable stance with your feet wide apart

1 Position a cable pulley above shoulder height and set the weight on the stack. Stand sideways and reach across with a double-handed grip on the stirrup handle.

Keep your outside shoulder higher than your inside shoulder

Pull the cable smoothly toward your inside hip

3 Keep pulling the handle down and around in a smooth motion, allowing your knees and hips to rotate a little.

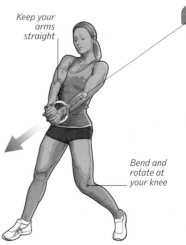

Keep your arms straight

Bend and rotate at your knee

4 Keep your arms straight and continue the rotation. Ensure that your shoulders are in line with your hips and that your head is facing your hands.

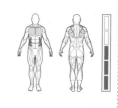

Look in the direction of your hands

Keep your trunk upright

Pivot on the ball of your foot

2 Start to pull the handle down and across your body toward your inside hip, as if felling a tree with an axe. Rotate your body toward the midline.

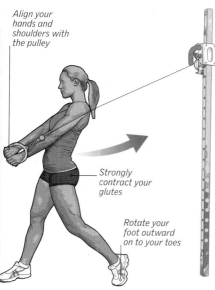

Align your hands and shoulders with the pulley

Strongly contract your glutes

Rotate your foot outward on to your toes

5 Rotate until your head, hips, shoulders, and hands are in line. Return to the start position, complete your set and repeat on the other side.

VARIATION

Try using a straight bar attachment instead of the stirrup handle. Begin facing away from the pulley, your feet hip-width apart. With your arms straight, rotate toward the pulley, keeping your feet firmly in place. At the end of the movement, you should be looking over your shoulder toward the pulley. Pull down, keeping your arms straight, until your near hand becomes level with your opposite hip.

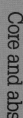

Core and abs

Side bend

Side bends are the easiest way to work your obliques—the muscles that help to stabilize your core and maintain the good posture needed to get the most benefit from other resistance exercises. Obliques are involved in movements that demand rotational strength, typical of most sports that include throwing.

1 Stand upright with your knees slightly bent and one dumbbell resting on the side of your thigh. Keep your weighted arm straight.

Rest your fingertips on your temples to help align your body

Keep your feet flat on the floor throughout

Move your torso laterally, not forward or backward

Contract your obliques to straighten your torso

Lower the dumbbell to knee level

Keep your knees slightly bent

2 Lean slowly sideways and slide the dumbbell down your thigh to knee level while breathing in. Do not allow the weight to swing.

3 Straighten your torso by contracting your obliques on the opposite side to the weight. Breathe out as you move to the upright position.

Core and abs

Suitcase deadlift

This underused exercise works not only your legs but your whole body. As its name suggests, this is a deadlift rather than a side bend, so remember to move your body as a unit and not to flex your trunk.

1 Adopt the get-set position with the kettlebell outside your foot, your hips above your knees, and your back flat and tight.

Keep your shoulder vertically above the weight

Make sure your working arm is straight

Turn out your feet and keep them in line with your knees

> ❝ THIS IS A **DEADLIFT THAT WORKS** NOT ONLY YOUR LEGS, BUT THE **WHOLE BODY**. ❞

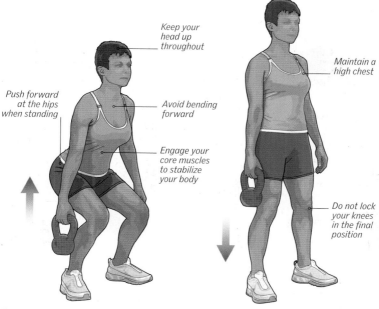

Keep your head up throughout

Push forward at the hips when standing

Avoid bending forward

Engage your core muscles to stabilize your body

Maintain a high chest

Do not lock your knees in the final position

2 Maintaining good posture throughout, drive up strongly with your legs: imagine that you are pushing your feet into the floor.

3 Stand up straight with the weight by the side of your thigh. Return to the start position and complete the set before switching sides.

Core and abs

The Cool-down

Upper-back stretch

This stretch specifically mobilizes the muscles in your upper back, making it useful across a range of sports, particularly those that involve throwing.

Interlock your fingers, palms facing away from you. Bring your hands to chest level and extend your arms, locking out your elbows and pushing your shoulders forward.

Push your arms forward, feeling the stretch in your upper back

Shoulder stretch

This easy and effective stretch specifically works the muscles around your shoulder joint. It is useful for weightlifters and those engaged in throwing events.

Extend one arm across your body and place your other forearm over its elbow. Apply gentle pressure until you feel tension in the shoulder of your extended arm. Repeat on the other side.

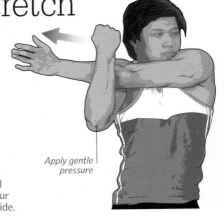

Apply gentle pressure

Erector stretch

This stretch works the erector spinae muscles that run on either side of your spine from the back of your head to your pelvis.

Pull your knees gently toward your chest

Lie back on an exercise mat. Bring your knees toward your chest and wrap your arms around them. Pull gently until you feel the stretch tension in your back.

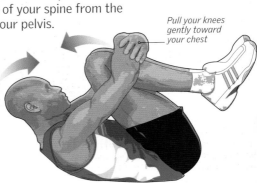

ITB stretch

The iliotibial band (ITB) is a band of connective tissue that runs down the outside of your thigh. Runners, hikers, gymnasts, and dancers should perform this stretch regularly to help prevent inflammation of the area above the knee—a common cause of pain.

Stand upright with your feet hip-width apart. Bring one leg across the other while at the same time raising your opposite arm above your head for balance. You should feel tension in the outside of your rear leg. Repeat on the other side.

VARIATION

Sit on the floor with your legs extended. Bend one leg and cross it over your extended leg so that your foot is flat on the floor. Supporting yourself with one arm, reach over with your free hand and gently press on the outside of your knee until you can feel the stretch in your ITB.

Bring your front leg across

Lat stretch

Specifically targeting the latissimus dorsi muscles, this stretch is useful for weightlifters, rowers, and field athletes.

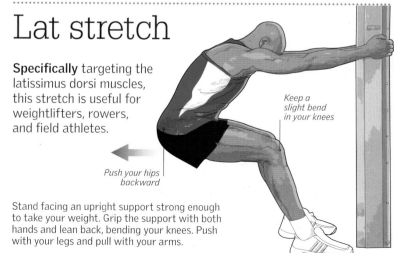

Keep a slight bend in your knees

Push your hips backward

Stand facing an upright support strong enough to take your weight. Grip the support with both hands and lean back, bending your knees. Push with your legs and pull with your arms.

3-point quad stretch

The purpose of this stretch is to work the quadriceps muscles on the front of your upper thigh and promote flexibility at your knee joint. Relatively simple to perform, it is useful following any type of leg workout.

Keep your body upright

Keep your hips in line with your shoulders

Rest the top of your foot on the bench

Bend your knee to an angle of about 90 degrees

Keep your head up

Feel the stretch in your quads

1 Stand up facing away from a bench or other suitable support. Bend one knee and place your foot on the support.

2 Bend your supporting leg slowly, lowering your body until you can feel the stretch in your opposite thigh.

Flex at the ankle

Push up to return, working your calf muscles strongly

> THIS STATIC STRETCH WORKS THE **QUADRICEPS MUSCLES** OF YOUR UPPER THIGH.

3 Push up with your supporting leg to return to the start position. Be sure to repeat the stretch on your other leg.

Hamstring stretch 1

Activity that involves repeated knee flexion, such as running or cycling, can cause tightness in your hamstrings. This stretch helps you to protect this vulnerable area.

Lie on your back with your legs extended. Lift each leg in turn, keeping the knee braced and the toes pulled back toward your body. Feel the stretch in your hamstrings. If you can, pull back on your leg a little and extend the stretch.

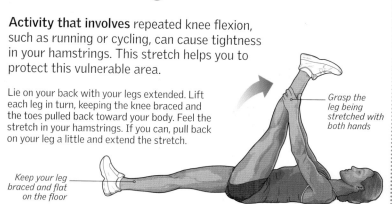

Grasp the leg being stretched with both hands

Keep your leg braced and flat on the floor

Hamstring stretch 2

This is a simple all-purpose stretch that works all the muscles in your hamstrings, relieving the tightness that can stress your lower back. Stretch slowly and do not "bounce" at full extension.

Lie on your back with your legs extended. Bend one knee and gently bring it toward your chest until you feel the stretch. Feel the stretch in your hamstrings.

Grasp your leg just below your knee

Keep your head against the floor

Hamstring stretch 3

You can perform this version of the hamstring stretch in a small space, on a track, or at a competition venue.

Start by stepping forward with one foot and then bend your supporting leg. Keep your lead leg braced and both feet flat on the floor. Tilt your pelvis slightly forward. Hold for a few seconds, then switch sides.

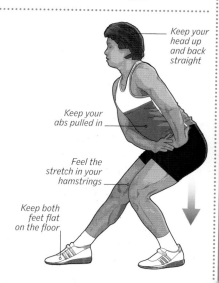

Keep your head up and back straight

Keep your abs pulled in

Feel the stretch in your hamstrings

Keep both feet flat on the floor

Quad stretch 1

Stretching the large muscles at the front of your thigh helps prevent injuries and reduce soreness. This stretch can be performed one leg at a time, or with both legs together.

Lie face down on a mat and bend one leg at your knee. Reach back with your hand on the same side, grasp your ankle, and pull back to feel the stretch in your quads.

Pull gently on your leg

Keep your back flat, not arched up

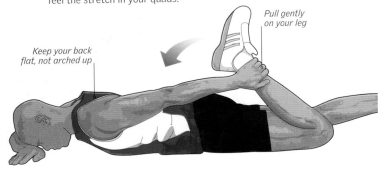

Quad stretch 2

This advanced stretch calls for good hip flexibility. It is a dual-purpose stretch that also works the adductor muscles on the insides of your thighs.

Sit with your trunk upright. Turn your feet in so that their soles touch. Reach forward with your hands and hold your feet together.

Push your knees gently down toward the floor

Feel the stretch in your quads

Adductor stretch 1

Stretching your adductor or groin muscles is key to maintaining hip flexibility for many sports.

Keep your body upright and your hands on your hips. Bend your lead leg so that your front knee can stay over your foot. Keep the trailing leg extended with your foot flat. Rock gently to the side.

Keep your body upright

Feel the stretch in your adductors

Keep your foot flat on the ground

Adductor stretch 2

This advanced version of the adductor stretch requires more agility to achieve the extended position: it is ideal for gymnasts and hurdlers.

Squat down on both legs; then move one leg out, resting it on the heel of your foot. "Sit in" to apply stretch to your adductors, but do not "bounce."

Pull your toes back toward your body

Feel the stretch in your adductors

Hamstring stretch

Tightness in your glutes often manifests itself as lower back pain after a workout. This fairly advanced stretch works your glutes as well as the muscles of your lower back and your hamstrings.

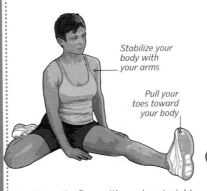

Stabilize your body with your arms

Pull your toes toward your body

Flex your trunk forward from your hips

Grasp your upper foot

Feel the stretch in your hamstrings

1 Sit on the floor with one leg straight ahead of you and one bent behind, keeping your hips and shoulders in line.

2 Lean forward gradually to your extended foot. Now grab your foot, and pull it gently toward yourself.

Calf stretch

Tight calf muscles are prone to injury during movements like sprinting, so this easy stretch is a must if you are a runner.

From a standing position, take a good step forward. Keep your feet hip-width apart. Bend the leading leg, keeping your knee over your foot.

Feel the stretch in your calf muscles

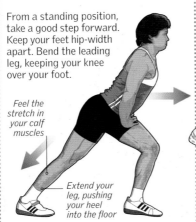

Extend your leg, pushing your heel into the floor

Pike calf stretch

The muscles of your calf—the gastrocnemius and the deeper soleus—are stretched in this advanced movement.

Feel the stretch in your calf muscles

Keep your hips high

Push your heel down into the floor

Take up a pike position. Place your right foot behind your left ankle. Keeping your legs straight, press the heel of your left foot down. Repeat on the other side.

Walking lunge stretch

This is a highly effective but simple multipurpose stretching exercise that mobilizes the whole of your hip area.

Keep your head level

Keep your trunk upright

Keep your upper leg parallel to the floor

Feel the stretch in your hips

Push off with your trailing leg

1 Stand with your feet hip-width apart and shoulders, hips, and feet in line.

2 Now take a long step forward. Drop down and bend at your knees.

Take a long step forward with your trailing leg

Step forward so that your knee is over your foot

Raise the ball of your foot

3 Step through with your trailing leg. Keep your body upright and head up.

4 Step forward and change legs, maintaining your body posture.

Programs

Introduction

The training programs in this section have been designed to help you get the best out of your training, whatever your gender, age, experience, strength, or goal. These programs cover three main resistance-training goals—bodybuilding, body sculpting, and strength. Basic programs are provided for each. Using a small number of targeted exercises, you can complete each session in about 30–40 minutes, and reduce the chance of you overtraining.

Q | WHAT CAN I EXPECT FROM THE PROGRAMS?

A | The featured programs allow you to tailor your training to help you realize your goals: this approach enables you to achieve the best possible results.

The programs in this section provide free-weight, body weight, and resistance machine variants, and none are too long. The days of dozens of obscure exercises are gone. Sports scientists recognize that simple and functional programs organized with specificity in mind and performed around 2–3 times per week, are a far more effective way to reach your goals.

Where possible, the programs are also designed with high levels of "functionality" (see p.23) in mind. This means that the exercises are applicable to real-life movements, either at home, at work, or in the sporting arena, as opposed to working single muscles in isolation. These exercises move your body in the way it was designed to move, so that you get better results, faster.

Q | WHAT ARE THE DIFFERENCES BETWEEN TRAINING WITH FREE WEIGHTS, BODY WEIGHT, AND RESISTANCE MACHINES?

A | Free weights offer you the highest level of "functionality" of the three. This is because free weights enable you to perform exercises that closely replicate "real life" movements, without the support and uniformity provided by resistance machines. Unsupported, your body engages additional smaller muscles in order to stabilize you—thus working more muscles than those you are specifically targeting, and offering you "added value" from your workout.

> ❝❝ THE EXERCISES **MOVE YOUR BODY** IN THE WAY IT WAS DESIGNED TO MOVE, SO THAT YOU GET **BETTER RESULTS**. ❞❞

BASIC PRINCIPLES

	Regardless of the program you follow, some basic training principles always apply:
Overload	Your training should demand more of your muscles than would normally be the case for everyday activity.
Recovery	An essential component in any training regimen, recovery literally means rest. It is while your body is resting that it adapts and strengthens, ready to be overloaded again during the next training session.
Progression	Your body adapts to the demands being placed on it. If you do not place extra demands on it, your training results will reach a plateau. So you have to gradually (and carefully) increase the number of sets, reps, and weight (or a combination of all three) to see continual progress.

Using your own bodyweight is another highly functional and effective way of developing strength, especially since it means you can train on the move, with little or no equipment. However, the disadvantage is that this form of training is obviously limited by the weight of your own body. Do not assume, however, that you will find using your body weight easier than other exercise methods.

Resistance machines provide you with padded body supports and enable you to perform exercises in a seated position; this means that you tend to work the targeted muscles in isolation. They can be a useful tool for those who are starting out, and even for those who want to work specific muscles. The machine-based exercises included in these programs have been chosen because they offer maximum functionality.

Q | WHY SHOULD I WARM UP AND COOL DOWN?

A | Warming up your muscles is essential because it gets your body ready for your workout while minimizing the risk of injury and maximizing your potential to learn and improve. Also, cooling down is equally important, since it returns your body to a resting state in a controlled manner. So do not be tempted to skip your warm-up before your training session or your cool-down at the end of the session, since this will increase your risk of injury and decrease your ability to complete your next workout without the restrictions and discomfort caused by tight and aching muscles.

• A good basic warm-up comprises 10 minutes of skipping, jogging, or working on the cross-trainer, followed by 10 minutes of warm-up stretches (pp.36–49). You can always tailor your warm-up if you need something more specific. A certified coach or fitness instructor can advise you.

• Cooling down can be achieved by 5–10 minutes of gentle jogging or walking. This decreases body temperature and heart rate and helps your muscles get rid of waste products such as lactic acid.

• Finally, perform 5–10 minutes of stretches, which help your muscles to relax and your muscle fibers to realign and re-establish their normal resting length and ranges of movement (see pp.146–53).

WARNING

Never do more than the programs suggest—you may overtrain, which can lead to illness and injury. Always consult your health-care practitioner before starting to train (see p.176).

UNDERSTANDING THE CHARTS

These are the terms you need to understand to use the charts effectively:

Sets	A group of repetitions, for example, two sets of five repetitions.
Repetitions	The number of times a weight should be lifted—"reps" for short.
Weight	The weight to be lifted, expressed as a RM figure. 1RM, for example, means a weight that you can lift only once. 12RM, means a weight that you can lift 12 times before muscular failure.
Muscular failure	This is the point at which you cannot perform another repetition of an exercise within a set.
Duration of program	A range is given for the number of weeks the program should be followed. You should not exceed this number.
Frequency of program	This is the number of workouts you should do per week, with the number of rest days you should take between workouts.
Recovery time	This is the amount of rest time in seconds or minutes that you should take between exercises.

Core strength program

The "core" (or "trunk") refers to the muscles found in your midsection. For many people, this is the sought-after "six pack" of abdominal muscles. In effect, there are two layers of core muscles; the superficial ones (such as your Rectus abdominus) that are visible in a lean individual, and the deep stabilizers, which are buried deeper in your trunk and which we cannot see.

Q | WHAT DO THE CHARTS SHOW?
A | The charts show two types of program—the first works the core muscles in isolation, the second adopts a more integrated approach.

Q | WHAT DOES THE ISOLATED CORE PROGRAM DO?
A | The core is seen as a separate area, which must be trained and strengthened using specific exercises. Start by completing 1–2 sets of 10 reps for each exercise. Add two reps to each exercise, every session, until you are completing two sets of 50 reps. Do not add additional reps if you are not ready.

Q | WHAT DO THE FUNCTIONAL CORE PROGRAMS DO?
A | Favored by many elite coaches, integrated core conditioning is the training of the core through other movements with the objective of enhancing the overall performance of that key movement, and not just to develop a strong core as an end in itself.

Q | WHICH ONE SHOULD I CHOOSE?
A | The functional core programs are the best. Everyone can learn to perform exercises such as squats, cleans, snatches, and deadlifts. The isolated core program approach is less functional and is good for physique development or bodybuilding where isolating a muscle and making it grow is the desired result.

ISOLATED CORE PROGRAM

Warm-up stretches (pp.36–49) 10 mins

EXERCISE	SETS	REPS
Abs crunch or **sit-up** (see pp.126–27) **(floor** or **stability ball)** (see p.135)	1–2	10–50
Reverse crunch (see p.128)	1–2	10–50
Figure-4 crunch (see p.130)	1–2	10–50
Ball jackknife (see p.139)	1–2	10–50
Side bend (see p.142)	1–2	10–50
V-leg raise (see p.131)	1–2	10–50
Prone plank (see p.132)	1	NMF*
Side plank (see p.133)	1	NMF*

COOL-DOWN ROUTINE

Cool-down 5 mins

Developmental stretching (pp.146–53) 15 mins

DURATION OF PROGRAM 4–6 weeks

FREQUENCY OF PROGRAM
2–3 workouts/week, 1–2 days' rest between workouts

RECOVERY TIME
2–5 minutes between exercises

*NMF—Near Muscular Failure

FUNCTIONAL CORE PROGRAMS

OPTION 1
Warm-up stretches (pp.36–49) 10 mins

EXERCISE	SETS	REPS	WEIGHT (RM)
Power clean (pp.122–23)	2–6	6	6
Standing pulley row (see p.68)	2–6	6	6
Barbell bench press (see p.58)	2–6	6	6
Bent-over row (see pp.74–75)	2–6	6	6
Military barbell press (see p.98)	2–6	6	6
Front barbell squat (see p.111)	2–6	6	6
Barbell deadlift (see pp.112–13)	2–6	6	6

COOL-DOWN ROUTINE

Cool-down 5 mins

Developmental stretching (pp.146–53) 15 mins

DURATION OF PROGRAM 4–6 weeks

FREQUENCY OF PROGRAM
2–3 workouts/week, 1–2 days' rest between workouts

RECOVERY TIME
2–5 minutes between exercises

FUNCTIONAL CORE PROGRAMS

OPTION 2
Warm-up stretches (pp.36–49) 10 mins

EXERCISE	SETS	REPS	WEIGHT (RM)
Power snatch (see pp.124–25)	2–6	6	6
Push-up (see p.52)	2–6	6	6
One-arm row (see p.73)	2–6	6	6
Suitcase deadlift (see p.143)	2–6	6	6
Back squat (see p.110)	2–6	6	6
Overhead barbell lunge (see p.114)	2–6	6	6
Straight-leg deadlift (see p.115)	2–6	6	6

COOL-DOWN ROUTINE

Cool-down 5 mins

Developmental stretching (pp.146–53) 15 mins

DURATION OF PROGRAM 4–6 weeks

FREQUENCY OF PROGRAM
2–3 workouts/week, 1–2 days' rest between workouts

RECOVERY TIME
2–5 minutes between exercises

Muscular endurance program

At a basic level, strength training ensures that we are strong enough to meet daily demands without fatigue or injury.

Q | WHAT WILL I ACHIEVE?
A | The programs are designed to develop strength endurance—the ability to move a relatively small weight through a specific range of motion lots of times.

Q | WHAT DO THE CHARTS SHOW?
A | They feature three programs, using resistance machines, bodyweight, or free weights. Depending on your preference, experience, and equipment available, choose one type of training. Do not try to do exercises on an ad hoc basis.

Q | HOW DO I FOLLOW THE CHARTS?
A | Work through each program from the top down, after warming up. Each exercise includes the number of sets, reps, and amount of weight you should use, followed by a cool-down routine. The weight you should use is expressed as your personal RM (Rep Maximum) or as NMF (Near Muscular Failure). The approximate duration, frequency of each program, and recovery time between each set is also provided.

Q | HOW WILL I PROGRESS?
A | Two key concepts in resistance training are overload and progression. Once you can complete a set easily, you can slightly increase the weight you are using, such as 2–5lb (1–2kg) for the upper body and 5–8lb (2–4kg) for the lower body, or add up to a maximum of 20 reps for each set. You can also reduce your recovery time by five seconds if starting at one minute's rest between exercises or sets. Do not go below 30 seconds rest. At the end of the six-week period, review your progress, and decide whether you should move on to one of the other programs.

MACHINE			
Moblization warm-up (pp.36–49) 10 mins			
EXERCISE	SETS	REPS	WEIGHT (RM)
Machine bench press (see p.54)	2–3	12+	12
Seated pulley row (see p.67) or **Machine fly** (see p.55)	2–3	12+	12
Upright row (see pp.100–01)	2–3	12+	12
Lat pull-down (see p.69)	2–3	12+	12
45-degree leg press (see p.106)	2–3	12+	12
Calf raise (see p.107)	2–3	12+	12
COOL-DOWN ROUTINE			
Cool-down 5 mins			
Developmental stretching (pp.146–53) 15 mins			
DURATION OF PROGRAMS 6 weeks			
FREQUENCY OF PROGRAMS 3 workouts/week, 1–2 days' rest between workouts			
RECOVERY TIME 30 secs–1 min between exercises			

BODY WEIGHT		
Moblization warm-up (pp. 36–49) 10 mins		
EXERCISE	SETS	WEIGHT
Push-up (see p.52)	2–3	NMF*
Chin-up (see pp.64–65) or Assisted chin-up (see p.70)	2–3	NMF*
Squat (see p.104)	2–3	NMF*
Reverse crunch (see p.128)	2–3	NMF*
Prone plank (see p.132)	2–3	NMF*
Side plank (see p.133)	2–3	NMF*
Sit-up (see p.127)	2–3	NMF*
COOL-DOWN ROUTINE		
Cool-down 5 mins		
Developmental stretching (pp.146–53) 15 mins		

DURATION OF PROGRAMS 6 weeks

FREQUENCY OF PROGRAMS
3 workouts/week, 1–2 days' rest between workouts

RECOVERY TIME
30 secs–1 min between exercises

FREE WEIGHT			
Moblization warm-up (pp. 36-49) 10 mins			
EXERCISE	SETS	REPS	WEIGHT (RM)
Back squat (see p.110)	2–3	12+	12
Dumbbell bench press (see p.59)	2–3	12+	12
Chin-up (Var.) (see p.65)	2–3	12+	12
Dumbbell shoulder press (see p.99)	2–3	12+	12
One-arm row (see p.73)	2–3	12+	12
Barbell deadlift (see pp.112–13)	2–3	12+	12
COOL-DOWN ROUTINE			
Cool-down 5 mins			
Developmental stretching (pp.146–53) 15 mins			

DURATION OF PROGRAMS 6 weeks

FREQUENCY OF PROGRAMS
3 workouts/week, 1–2 days' rest between workouts

RECOVERY TIME
30 secs–1 min between exercises

*NMF—Near Muscular Failure

Body sculpting program

Many people who take up resistance training want a better "physique." By this, they imagine more muscle and better muscle definition provided by larger muscles and reduced body fat levels.

Q | WHAT IS THE FREE WEIGHT "MIX AND MATCH" CHART?

A | The "mix and match" chart divides the exercises by body part. You can create your own program by choosing one exercise from each body part section, and perform the stated number of sets and reps. You can also swap exercises for each training session. The chart starts with a warm-up and finishes with a cool-down.

MACHINE			
Mobilization warm-up (pp.36–49) 10 mins			
EXERCISE	SETS	REPS	WEIGHT (RM)
Machine bench press or **Machine fly*** (see pp.54–55)	3–6	6–12	12
Seated pulley row (see p.67)	3–6	6–12	12
Dumbbell shoulder press (see p.99) or **Upright row*** (see pp.100–01)	3–6	6–12	12
Lat pull-down (see p.69)	3–6	6–12	12
Triceps push-down (see p.82)	3–6	6–12	12
Machine leg extension (see p.108) or **45-degree leg press*** (see p.106)	3–6	6–12	12
Calf raise (see p.107)	3–6	6–12	12
Pulley curl (see p.80) or **Reverse pulley curl*** (see p.81)	3–6	6–12	12

BODY WEIGHT		
Mobilization warm-up (pp.36–49) 10 mins		
EXERCISE	SETS	WEIGHT (RM)
Push-up (see p.52)	3–6	NMF*
Chin-up (see pp.64–65) or **Assisted chin-up** (see p.70)	3–6	NMF*
Squat (see p.104)	3–6	NMF*
Bar dip (see p.79)	3–6	NMF*
Reverse crunch (see p.128)	3–6	NMF*
Prone plank (see p.132)	3–6	NMF*
Side plank (see p.133)	3–6	NMF*
Sit-up (see p.127)	3–6	NMF*

COOL-DOWN ROUTINE FOR MACHINE AND BODY WEIGHT PROGRAMS

Cool-down 5 mins	**DURATION OF PROGRAM** 6–8 weeks **FREQUENCY OF PROGRAM** 3 workouts/week, 2 days' rest between workouts
Developmental stretching (pp.146–53) 15 mins	**RECOVERY TIME** 30 secs–1 min, 30 secs between exercises

*Alternate every session

*NMF—Near Muscular Failure

FREE WEIGHT "MIX AND MATCH"

Mobilization warm-up (pp.36–49) 10 mins

EXERCISE	SETS	REPS	WEIGHT (RM)
BACK EXERCISES (Choose one...)			
One-arm row (see p.73)	3–6	6–12	12–14
Bent-over row (see pp.74–75)	3–6	6–12	12–14
Lat pull-down (see p.69)	3–6	6–12	12–14
Barbell pull-over (see pp.76–77)	3–6	6–12	12–14
LOWER BACK EXERCISES (Choose one...)			
Good morning barbell (see p.121)	3–6	6–12	12–14
Straight-leg deadlift (see p.115)	3–6	6–12	12–14
Back extension (see p.66)	3–6	6–12	12–14
Ball back extension (see p.137)	3–6	6–12	12–14
TRUNK EXERCISES (Choose one...)			
Abs crunch or sit-up (see pp.126–27)	3–6	6–12	12–14
V-leg raise (see p.131)	3–6	6–12	12–14
Prone plank (see p.132)	3–6	6–12	12–14
Side plank (see p.133)	3–6	6–12	12–14
LEG EXERCISES (Choose one...)			
Back squat (see p.110)	3–6	6–12	12–14
Front barbell squat (see p.111)	3–6	6–12	12–14
Forward lunge (see p.105) or Dumbbell split squat (see p.116)	3–6	6–12	12–14
Barbell step-up (see pp.118–19)	3–6	6–12	12–14

EXERCISE	SETS	REPS	WEIGHT (RM)
SHOULDER EXERCISES (Choose one...)			
Dumbbell shoulder press (see p.99)	3–6	6–12	12–14
Upright row (Var.) (see pp.100–01)	3–6	6–12	12–14
Military barbell press (see p.98)	3–6	6–12	12–14
TRICEPS EXERCISES (Choose one...)			
Dumbbell/Barbell triceps extension (see pp.90–91)	3–6	10–12	12–14
Close-grip bench press (see pp.92–93)	3–6	10–12	12–14
Triceps push-down (see p.82)	3–6	10–12	12–14
Bench or bar dip (see pp.78–79)	3–6	10–12	12–14
CHEST EXERCISES (Choose one...)			
Dumbbell bench press (see p.59)	3–6	6–12	12–14
Barbell bench press (see p.58)	3–6	6–12	12–14
Incline fly (see pp.62–63)	3–6	6–12	12–14

COOL-DOWN ROUTINE

Cool-down 5 mins

Developmental stretching (pp.146–53) 15 mins

DURATION OF PROGRAM 8 weeks

FREQUENCY OF PROGRAM 3 workouts/week, 2 days' rest between workouts

RECOVERY TIME 30 secs–1 min, 30 secs between exercises

Bodybuilding program

Bodybuilding is the process of enhancing muscle mass to the greatest possible extent. It is also about reducing body fat so that the muscle clearly shows through the skin. Bodybuilding is both a method of improving physical appearance as well as a competitive sport—its most famous champion being the former Mr. Universe and Mr. Olympia, Arnold Schwarzenegger.

WARNING

You need to be very realistic about how much muscle mass you can develop without straining yourself, since only a few people are genetically suited to seriously bulking up. In fact, a genetically average individual, who is training naturally, would severely overtrain if they attempted to follow the programs of elite bodybuilders. Even if they could cope with the training without physiologically breaking down, they would still struggle to gain muscle mass. This happens because most people's muscles simply cannot recover quickly enough between overly frequent and intense sessions, let alone grow in size.

Q | WHAT DO THE PROGRAM CHARTS SHOW?

A | The programs outlined in the chart are founded on high-intensity, abbreviated bodybuilding training. The programs discussed in this book offer a choice of highly effective programs that use either resistance machines or free weights.

❝ BODYBUILDING HELPS **ENHANCE MUSCLE MASS** TO THE MAXIMUM POSSIBLE EXTENT. IT ALSO **REDUCES BODY FAT**. **❞**

Q | HOW DO I USE THE PROGRAMS?

A | The programs provide whole-body workouts. Ideally, you should work through each of the training programs from the top down, after you have warmed up your muscles. Each of the featured exercises include a page reference to its step-by-step instruction in the book. This is followed by the number of sets, reps, and amount of weight you should use, followed by a cool-down routine. The weight you should use for each exercise is expressed in terms of your personal RM (Rep Maximum) for the machines and free weights. The duration, the frequency of each program, and the recovery time between each set of exercises is also provided at the bottom of the chart.

Q | SHOULD I TRAIN HARDER TO BUILD MORE MUSCLE?

A | No. The key to successful bodybuilding is to train smarter, not harder. It is more common to see well-meaning, passionate bodybuilding trainees doing too much rather than too little.

Q | WHY ARE THERE NO BODYWEIGHT EXERCISES?

A | There are no bodyweight exercises included in any of the bodybuilding programs because it is very difficult to increase the amount of weight you are lifting—you are limited to the weight of your own body, which is not sufficient for this type of resistance training.

MACHINE

Moblization warm-up
(pp.36–49) 10 mins

EXERCISE	SETS	REPS	WEIGHT (RM)
Machine bench press (see p.54)	3–6	6–12	12
Seated pulley row (see p.67)	3–6	6–12	12
Dumbbell shoulder press (see p.99) or **Upright row** (see pp.100–01)	3–6	6–12	12
Lat pull-down (see p.69)	3–6	6–12	12
45-degree leg press (see p.106)	3–6	6–12	12
Pulley curl (see p.80)	3–6	6–12	12
Triceps push-down (see p.82) or **Bar dip** (see p.79)	3–6	6–12	12

COOL-DOWN ROUTINE

Cool-down 5 mins

Developmental stretching (pp.146–53) 15 mins

DURATION OF PROGRAM 6–8 weeks

FREQUENCY OF PROGRAM
2–3 workouts/week, 1–2 days' rest between workouts

RECOVERY TIME
30 secs–1 min
30 secs between exercises

FREE WEIGHT

Moblization warm-up
(pp.36–49) 10 mins

EXERCISE	SETS	REPS	WEIGHT (RM)
Close-grip bench press (see pp.92–93)	3–6	6–12	12
Back squat (see p.110)	3–6	6–12	12
Bent-over row (see pp.74–75)	3–6	6–12	12
Incline fly (see pp.62–63)	3–6	6–12	12
Chin-up (wide grip) (Var.) (see p.65)	3–6	6–12	12
Military barbell press (see p.98)	3–6	6–12	12
Barbell curl (see p.86)	3–6	6–12	12

COOL-DOWN ROUTINE

Cool-down 5 mins

Developmental stretching (pp.146–53) 15 mins

DURATION OF PROGRAM 6–8 weeks

FREQUENCY OF PROGRAM
2–3 workouts/week, 1–2 days' rest between workouts

RECOVERY TIME
30 secs–1 min
30 secs between exercises

Maximal strength program

The following program will help you to develop a high level of strength from head to toe—enabling you to perform any real-world movement that may ever be asked of you—through a series of functional exercises. It builds on the muscle endurance program given on pp.160–61 and will build your strength over an eight-week period.

Q | WHAT DOES THE PROGRAM CHART SHOW?

A | The chart shows a basic but highly effective whole-body program. The program is effective in achieving your strength goals. Each of the featured exercises includes a page reference to its step-by-step instruction in the main part of the book. This is followed by the number of sets, reps, and amount of weight you should use, followed by a cool-down routine. The approximate duration, frequency of each program, and the recovery time between each set of exercises is provided.

Q | HOW DO I FOLLOW THE PROGRAM?

A | Begin the cycle by lifting a weight that is challenging for six repetitions, but allows comfortable completion of all sets. The goal of the program is to progress toward lifting the largest weight you can, once only. Every two weeks, the number of repetitions decreases, but with a weekly increase of weight: 2lb–5lb (1–2.5kg) upper body; 5lb–8lb (2–4kg) lower body. You should be aiming to lift the largest amount of weight once in the final week—week eight.

WHOLE-BODY PROGRAM

Mobilization warm-up (pp.36–49) 10 mins

EXERCISE	SETS	REPS	WEIGHT (RM)
Dumbbell bench press (see p.59)	3	6	6
Back squat (see p.110)	3	6	6
Lat pull-down (see p.69)	3	6	6
Military barbell press (see p.98)	3	6	6
Bent-over row (see pp.74–75)	3	6	6

LOADS AND INTENSITIES

WEEK	SETS	REPS	WEIGHT (RM)
Weeks 1–2	3	6	6
Weeks 3–4	3	4	4
Weeks 5–6	4	3	3
Weeks 7–8	4	1–2	2

COOL-DOWN ROUTINE

Cool-down 5 mins

Developmental stretching (pp.146–53) 15 mins

DURATION OF PROGRAM 8 weeks

FREQUENCY OF PROGRAM 3 workouts/week, 2 days' rest between workouts

RECOVERY TIME 3–5 minutes between exercises

Sports-specific exercises

All the exercises in this book provide great strength training in themselves. However, a large proportion are also of great benefit for training for specific sports. Almost all athletes, regardless of their chosen sport, will spend time in the gym performing specific strengthening and conditioning exercises that will help them excel in their chosen field.

In the charts below, the most sports-specific exercises featured in the book are grouped together into "exercise groups." Use these charts in conjunction with the sports-specific matrix (see pp.168–69) to improve your performance in your chosen sport.

EXERCISE GROUPS

SQUATS

Back squat (p.110)
Front barbell squat (p.111)

SPLIT SQUATS AND LUNGES

Dumbbell split squat (p.116)
Overhead split squat (p.117)
Bulgarian barbell split squat (p.120)
Overhead barbell lunge (p.114)
Forward lunge (p.105)
Barbell step-up (pp.118–19)

DEADLIFTS

Barbell deadlift (pp.112–13)
Suitcase deadlift (p.143)
Straight-leg deadlift (p.115)
Good morning barbell (p.121)

PULL- AND CHIN-UPS

Assisted chin-up (p.70)
Lat pull-down (p.69)
Chin-up (pp.64–65)
Chin-up variable grip (p.65 var.)

EXERCISE GROUPS

PULLEY ROWS

Seated pulley row (p.67)
Standing pulley row (p.68)
Prone row (p.72)
One-arm row (p.73)
Bent-over row (p.74–75)
Upright row (pp.100–01)

SHOULDER/OVERHEAD PRESSES

Military barbell press (p.98)
Dumbbell shoulder press (p.99)

STRAIGHT-ARM PULLS

Barbell pull-over (pp.76–77)
Dumbbell pull-over (p.77 var.)
Straight-arm pull-down (p.71)

PRESSING MOVEMENTS: THE CHEST

Barbell bench press (p.58)
Dumbbell bench press (p.59)
Push-up (p.52)
Ball press-up (p.52 var.)
Frame-supported push-up (p.53)
Close-grip bench press (pp.92–93)
Close-grip press-up (p.93 var.)

> **THESE EXERCISES ARE USEFUL FOR ANYONE INTERESTED IN ENHANCING THEIR SPORTS PERFORMANCE.**

Sports-specific matrix

The term "sports-specific" is applied to exercises that mirror the particular movements of an athlete in their chosen sport. This allows you to break different sports down into their general movement types and train those movements to improve your overall level of performance.

KEY
On the right are the exercises from pp.50–143 grouped together into "exercise groups." Below are the sports they are relevant to. The key is:

■ Directly relevant
□ Partial/general relevance

	SQUATS	SPLIT SQUATS AND LUNGES	DEADLIFTS (BENT LEG)	DEADLIFTS (STRAIGHT LEG)	PULL- AND CHIN-UPS	SEATED PULLEY ROWS	STANDING ROWS	SHOULDER/OVERHEAD PRESSES	STRAIGHT-ARMS PULLS	PRESSING MOVEMENTS: THE CHEST
American Football	■	■	□	□	□	□	■	■		□
Australian Rules Football	■	■	□	□	□	□	■	□		□
Badminton	□	■			□	□	□	□	□	
Baseball/Softball	■	■			□	□	□	□		
Basketball	■	■		□	□	□	□	■		
Boxing	■	■			□	□	□	■		■
Canoeing			□		□	■	■		□	
Climbing	□	□	□		■	□	□			
Cricket	■	■			□	□	□		□	
Cycling	■	□	□							
Distance Running	■	■	□							
Fencing	□	■								
Field Hockey	■	■		□						
Gaelic Football	■	■			□	□	■	□		□
Golf	□	□				□	□	□		
Gymnastics	■	□	□		■	□	□	□	□	
Hammer	■	□	■	■	□		■	□		
Hurling	■	■			□	□	□	□		
Ice Hockey	■	■								
Ice Skating	□	□								
Javelin	■	■			□	□	□	□	□	
Judo	■	■	■	■	□	□	■	□		□
Jumping Sports	■	■		□						
Kayaking			□		□	■	■		□	

Q | WHAT DOES THE CHART SHOW?

A | The chart has been developed by analyzing the movement patterns of each of the sports listed here, and categorizing all the exercise groups given in this book by their relevance to those specific sports, as follows: "direct relevance" (gray square), "partial relevance" (clear square), or "no relevance" (blank). In the case of squash, for example, squats are of partial relevance, whereas split squats and lunges are of direct relevance. Although it is still important to develop your two-legged leg strength in squash at a foundation level (and hence the general relevance) single-leg strength is arguably more important and directly related, due to the explosive multidirectional movements you would make when accelerating or lunging for the ball.

KEY
On the right are the exercises from pp.50–143 grouped together into "exercise groups." Below are the sports they are relevant to. The key is:
■ Directly relevant
□ Partial/general relevance

	SQUATS	SPLIT SQUATS AND LUNGES	DEADLIFTS (BENT LEG)	DEADLIFTS (STRAIGHT LEG)	PULL- AND CHIN-UPS	SEATED PULLEY ROWS	STANDING ROWS	SHOULDER/OVERHEAD PRESSES	STRAIGHT-ARMS PULLS	PRESSING MOVEMENTS: THE CHEST
Lacrosse	■	■			□	□	□			
Middle Distance Running	■	■		□						
MMA	■	■	■	■	□	□	■	■		■
Netball	□	■						□		
Powerlifting	■		■	■	□	□	□	□	□	■
Rowing	■		■	□	□	■	■			
Rugby League	■	■	□	□	□	□	■	□		■
Rugby Union	■	■	■	□	□	□	■	■		■
Skiing	■	□								
Soccer	■	■		□						
Squash/Racketball	□	■			□	□	□	□	□	
Striking Martial Arts	■	■			□	□	□	■		■
Surfing	■	■								
Swimming	□	□		□	□	□	□	□	□	
Table Tennis		■								
Tennis	■	■			□	□	□	□		
Shot Putt & Discus	■	■	□	□	□	□	□	■		■
Sprints	■	■		□						
Volleyball	■	■			□	□	□	□	□	
Waterskiing	■			□	□	□	■			
Water Polo	□				□	□	□	□	□	
Weightlifting	■	■	■	□	□			□	■	□
Windsurfing	■		□		□	□	□			
Wrestling	■	■	■		□	□	■	□		■

Glossary

%1RM The load lifted in an exercise as a percentage of your *1RM* (*one repetition maximum*).

1RM (One Repetition Maximum) The maximum amount of weight that you can lift in a single repetition for a specific training exercise.

Abductor A muscle that functions to pull a limb away from your body.

Adductor A muscle that functions to pull a limb toward your body.

Anterior The front part or surface, as opposed to *posterior*.

Barbell A type of *free weight* made up of a bar (usually metal) with weights at both ends that is long enough for you to hold with at least a shoulder-width grip. The weights may be permanently attached to the bar or may be removable disks (plates) that are attached to the bar with a collar.

BER (Basic Energy Requirement) The number of *calories* expended by your body when you are at rest.

Biceps Any muscle that has two *heads* or origins, but commonly used as shorthand for the biceps brachii, which is located on your upper arm.

BMR (Basic Metabolic Rate) The minimum amount of energy (in *calories*) that your body needs daily to stay alive. BMR accounts for approximately two-thirds of your total daily energy expenditure.

Body fat percentage The weight of your body fat expressed as a percentage of total body weight.

BMI (Body Mass Index) A measure of body fat based on height and weight that applies to adult men and women. It is a useful measure for "average" people but should be interpreted with caution, especially when applied to athletes with considerable muscle bulk.

Cable pulley machine A resistance training machine in which various attachments, such as a bar, handle, or rope, can be linked to weights by a metal cable. The force for moving the weight is transferred via a pulley or system of pulleys. These machines are designed to offer many exercise options while providing continual resistance throughout the full range of motion of the exercise.

Calorie A commonly used unit of energy taken in or expended.

Carbohydrates A group of organic compounds, including sugar, starch, and cellulose. An essential part of your diet, carbohydrates are the most common source of energy in living things.

Cardiac muscle A type of involuntary muscle found in the walls of your heart.

Clean and Jerk A technical two-part lift that, with the *snatch* is one of the two Olympic weightlifting disciplines. It involves lifting a barbell to shoulder height, then jerking it overhead to arm's length.

Cool-down A period after completion of your main training session that includes activities such as slow jogging, walking, and stretching of your major muscle groups. It is designed to help return your body to its pre-exercise state.

Dumbbell A type of *free weight* made up of a short bar with a weight at each end. It can be lifted with one hand.

Erector A muscle that raises a body part.

Extensor A muscle that works to increase the angle at a joint—for example, straightening your elbow. It usually works in tandem with a *flexor*.

Fats A group of organic compounds, including animal fats, such as butter and lard, and vegetable fats, such as vegetable and bean oils. Fats are a significant source of energy in the diet and many play essential roles in your body's chemistry.

Flexor A muscle that works to decrease the angle at a joint—for example, bending your elbow. It usually works in tandem with an *extensor*.

Free weight A weight, usually a *barbell* or *dumbbell*, not tethered to a cable or machine.

GI (Glycemic Index) A way of quantifying the effect that taking in a particular type of *carbohydrate* food has on your blood sugar level on a scale of 0–100. High GI foods are those that break down quickly, releasing energy soon after digestion; low GI foods break down more slowly and release their energy over a longer period.

Head (of a muscle) The point of origin of a muscle.

Homeostasis The processes by which your body regulates its internal environment to keep conditions stable and constant.

ITB (Iliotibial Band) A tough group of fibers running along the outside of your thigh that primarily works as a stabilizer during running.

Lateral Positioned toward the outside of your body or a part of your body. Any kind of movement in the lateral plane refers to a side-to-side movement.

Ligament A tough and fibrous connective tissue that connects your bones together at your joints.

Metabolism The sum of all your body's chemical processes; it comprises anabolism (building up compounds) and catabolism (breaking down compounds).

Mineral Any one of many inorganic (non-carbon-based) elements that are essential for normal body function and that must be included in your diet.

Neutral spine The position of the spine that is considered to be good posture. In this posture, the spine is not completely straight, but has slight curves in its upper and lower regions. It is the strongest and most balanced position for the spine and needs to be maintained in many exercises.

Overload The progressive increase in weight used for a particular exercise. It is designed to promote adaptation of the body in response to training.

Posterior The back part or surface, as opposed to *anterior*.

Power The amount of force produced in a given time – a combination of strength and speed.

Powerlifting A sport in which the goal is to lift a *barbell* loaded with the heaviest possible weights; it consists of three events—the squat, the bench press, and the deadlift.

Protein One of the three main nutrients (along with *fats* and *carbohydrates*) that supply energy to your body. Protein is required for muscular growth and repair.

Quadriceps Any muscle with four heads, but most commonly used to describe the large muscle of your thigh.

Regimen A regulated course of exercise and diet designed to produce a pre-determined result.

Rest interval The pause between *sets* of an exercise that allows muscle recovery.

Repetition (rep) One complete movement of a particular exercise, from start to finish and back.

Resistance training Any type of training in which your muscles work against a resistance; the resistance may be provided by a weight, an elastic band, or your own bodyweight.

Set A specific number of *repetitions*.

Shoulder girdle The ring of bones (actually an incomplete ring) at your shoulder that provides an attachment point for the many muscles that allow your shoulder and elbow joints to move.

Snatch A technical lift that, along with the *clean and jerk*, is one of the two Olympic weightlifting disciplines. It involves lifting a *barbell* in one continuous movement from the ground (or more usually from a lifting platform) to a position where it is held overhead on your locked arms.

Strength training A form of *resistance training* in which your goal is to build the strength of your skeletal muscle.

Supplement Any preparation in the form of a powder, pill, or liquid that contains nutrients.

Tendon A type of connective tissue that joins your muscles to your bones, so transmitting the force of muscle contraction to your bones.

Triceps Any muscle with three *heads*, but commonly used as shorthand for the triceps brachii, which extends your elbow.

Vitamin Any one of a group of chemical compounds that is required by your body in small amounts for healthy growth and development. Most vitamins are not made by your body, so must be taken in the diet.

Warm-up A series of low-intensity exercises that prepares your body for a workout by moderately stimulating your heart, lungs, and muscles.

Index

Acknowledgments

About the authors

Len Williams is an International Weightlifting Referee and a Senior Coach for the British Weight Lifters' Association. He tutors at colleges and universities on various training courses. Len is currently in the squad of officials preparing for the 2012 Olympic games in London.

Derek Groves is a professional sports coach and a staff coach with the British Weight Lifters' Association and a Consultant Staff Coach to the Saudi Arabian Federation of Sport for Disability Powerlifting. He has over 30 years' experience in strength training and conditioning for elite athletes and is currently an International Classifier for IPC Paralympic Powerlifting.

Glen Thurgood is a professional BWLA coach and Head of Strength and Conditioning at Northampton Town Football Club. With over 10 years' combined experience as an elite athlete and coach, he has worked with rugby union, football, and baseball teams at university, professional, and national levels.

Publisher's acknowledgments

Dorling Kindersley would like to thank the following people for their help with the preparation of this book: Mike Garland, Mark Walker, Darren R. Awuah, Debajyoti Dutta, Richard Tibbitts, Jon Rogers, and Phil Gamble for the illustrations; Adam Brackenbury for creative technical support; and Margaret McCormack for indexing.

SAFETY INFORMATION

All sports and physical activity involves some risk of injury. Participants must take all reasonable care to ensure that they are free from any medical condition which could contra-indicate participation in weightlifting, weight training, or any other form of resistance exercise.

The publishers of this book and its contributors are confident that, when properly performed, weightlifting and weight training are safe, and that the exercises described in this book, correctly executed, with gradual increases in resistance and proper supervision, are also safe. However, it is incumbent upon users of weightlifting and weight training facilities to exercise sensible judgment, and to ensure that floors, equipment, ventilation, and hygiene are all fit for purpose.

Supervisors and coaches should carry adequate insurance and have relevant up-to-date qualifications, including first aid certfication.

Although sports scientists have worked to improve the knowledge underpinning the choice of resistance, the construction of training programs, and the many other variables considered when creating them, there remain very few absolutes. Different combinations of exercises, diverse ordering, and the variation of volumes and intensities, etc, may all work. The effectiveness of a schedule is markedly influenced by the individual using it, and the period of time before it is changed: coaches constantly observe athletes and vary programs whenever they appear to be losing effectiveness. In training for sports other than Olympic weightlifting, it is clearly essential that a strength and conditioning coach works closely with well informed coaches of that sport.

All current research shows that weightlifting and weight training is safe for children, in comparison with traditional school sports, but, for obvious reasons, children should always be particularly well supervised.

The publishers and authors of this book disclaim all responsibility for injury to persons or property consequent on embarking upon the exercises herein described.